UNBREAKABLE

Surviving Adversity

John Cullen

First printing edition 2023
Printed by IngramSpark in the United States of America
Book design by Nada Orlic

www.itsjustparkinsons.com

ISBN: 979-8-9891587-0-6

Legal Disclaimer:
The advice and strategies contained herein reflect the research and ideas of the author and are not intended to substitute for the services of a trained healthcare practitioner. Consult your healthcare practitioner before engaging in any diet, drug or exercise regimen. The author and the publisher disclaim responsibility for any adverse effects resulting directly or indirectly from the information contained in this book.

John's Disclaimer:
Don't act foolishly or impulsively when considering adopting any of this book's recommendations. The recommendations I make in this book work for me. They may not work for you. Do your homework before adopting any of my strategies. Consult your healthcare provider BEFORE doing anything in this book.

*This book is dedicated to
everyone facing adversity in their life.*

CONTENTS

Forward

Friends, strangers, and interviewers ask me all the time whom I admire. The list is long, from Stephen Hawking to Dolly Parton to Ukrainian President Volodymyr Zelenskyy. But the number one name on my list of those I profoundly admire is John Cullen.

Let's start with the expression, "Walk a Mile in My Shoes." John Cullen has been a tall, strong, physically tough man all his life. He has climbed mountains, cycled the Pyrenees, and crossed the United States via hitchhiking, among many challenging physical adventures. But on one specific day in 2015, Parkinson's came to John as an uncontrollable twitch in his right index finger. A few years later, the disease has transformed John's once-long stride into a stutter step. John needs to ask for help buttoning or unbuttoning his shirt. He occasionally can't pull his pants down for a visit to the toilet. Can we for a nanosecond imagine walking a mile in John's shoes?

John is educated and extremely knowledgeable about the ravages of Parkinson's. After all, he's living with those ravages, witnessing his own body decline almost day by day. Yet this brave man has made his stand. He is going to find a smile, going to put into perspective his love of living every day to his ultimate potential.

This beautiful book of his, *UNBREAKABLE*, doesn't use as its subtitle: *Surviving Parkinson's*. Sure, there are plenty of facts and therapies and much wisdom directed toward those who also live with Parkinson's, and their loved ones, but the book's subtitle is: *Surviving Adversity*.

With every mantra of John's, from "Never Give Up, Never Surrender" to "It's Just Parkinson's," there are countless pearls of wisdom for ALL of us to grab onto in this book. Page by page, you will find concepts to guide you toward purpose and joy. Every single one of us on planet earth will know heartache. We will suffer pain. When I lay down *UNBREAKABLE* after reading it thirstily cover to cover, I found myself with a new lease on life. I swelled with gratitude for the powers I do have, instead of focusing on the loves lost or the abilities waned or the missed opportunities.

John admits his eyes are wide open to the one-way street Parkinson's is taking him down. He will never reverse the disabilities he manages every day. He will only get worse, as far as physical capacities go. And it is poignant to read John's words about accepting the fact Parkinson's will eventually take his life.

But he point-blank refuses to accept defeat. He relishes every uplifting conversation. He applauds his fellow Parkinson's sufferers for their courage. John looks into every nook and cranny of life for positives. The final words of his poem at once chill my soul and fire my admiration. John writes, "I'm still here. I'm still me."

Bravo, John Cullen. Bravo for your UNBREAKABLE life force!

Diana Nyad
The first and only person to swim nonstop from Cuba to Florida in 2013: 110.86 miles in 52 hours and 54 minutes.
Los Angeles, USA
2023

Preface

Would you think I'm crazy if I told you that being diagnosed with Parkinson's disease has made my life better? What if I told you having an incurable, progressive, neurodegenerative disease has enriched my life in ways I could never have imagined? I bet you're wondering, *how is this possible?*

Here's the obvious: Parkinson's doesn't discriminate; like most diseases, it's happy to grab ahold of whoever it can. This also means Parkinson's doesn't care whether you're rich or poor, short or tall, fat or skinny; it's an equal opportunity destroyer of lives.

By not discriminating, Parkinson's afflicts a large, diverse group of people… but in the process, it also brings together a large, diverse group of people. And *people* are a big reason why I say having Parkinson's disease has made my life better. I feel an immediate connection whenever I meet someone with Parkinson's because we're bonded by our shared struggle. We are bound together in an epic battle for our lives. And if people are willing to hear from my experience, I want to share one message: *never give up, never surrender.*

Unfortunately, not everybody with Parkinson's is actively fighting the disease. The ones who have chosen to fight inspire me. Whether it's swimming the English Channel, participating in obstacle course races, running marathons, or just walking around their neighborhood block, I admire every individual who has the courage, grit, tenacity, and audacity to stand up against this beast. Despite insurmountable odds, they choose to fight. I think that's remarkable! If you're reading this and not fighting, then it's your time to be inspired and step the f**k up to your new reality.

At this stage of my life, everything I do is geared toward battling Parkinson's. Everything I do focuses on one simple message: fight and never give up. You've got to engage this monster every single day! I'm aware that not every day is going to be an epic battle. In war, for every epic battle there are many skirmishes that are never reported. The same is true about the war against Parkinson's; there'll be lots of skirmishes but that reality shouldn't deter you from joining the battle.

In 2019 I created the motto: *It's Just Parkinson's* (IJP). Over the years I've done a lot of physical training – coming up with the IJP mantra was a way of training my mind.

I'm aware some people may be surprised to hear someone who is battling Parkinson's say, "It's just Parkinson's." Words matter. I use the word battle purposely because it *is* a battle, and by saying, "It's Just Parkinson's" I am *taking back* control of my life.

By instilling the IJP mantra into my psyche, I am able to modify my thoughts, attitudes, and beliefs to optimize positive thinking. Like physical training, I've nurtured and honed this mindset over many years, it didn't just sprout overnight.

Over the years, the motto has turned into a movement. Today, IJP's mission is simple: to be the rock for those facing a battle, to provide light for those lost in the dark, and to give hope to those who feel defeated. ROCK – LIGHT – HOPE.

IJP has become a worldwide social movement. In its short existence, IJP has inspired many fellow Parkinson's sufferers to get off the couch and continue living. By choosing to battle Parkinson's they're choosing LIFE. I am proud that IJP has changed many people's outlook, inspired them to action, and provided a foundation for them to move forward.

I've seen the IJP mindset motivate people who had given up, to get back into the game. I've had countless people tell me they see themselves in my struggles.

But the IJP mantra and movement is not just for those living with Parkinson's disease (PD). I've heard from countless individuals who don't have PD who've told me IJP has helped them face many other life challenges (including PTSD, bankruptcy, and the breakup of relationships).

The IJP way of life has been embraced globally, with followers worldwide, including (but not limited to): the United States of America, Canada, England, Ireland, the Netherlands, Australia, Brazil, Kuwait, and Romania. Through word of mouth and social media, people from around the world are learning about the IJP ethos and embracing it as their own.

I wrote this book because many of you asked for guidance or advice. It was never my intention to be a spokesperson or ambassador for those living with Parkinson's disease, but I humbly hope my story will help or inspire others.

The pages of this book reveal some very personal, and at times painful, details about my life. I'm being completely open about my struggles and breakthroughs, and I'm putting myself in a vulnerable position in hopes of helping others. I want everyone reading this book to know I've faced many of the same battles you may be facing, and I'm not pulling any punches. My great hope is that by sharing my experience, it may help you navigate the minefield you're in, and help you find the best way through it.

There are many ways to face Parkinson's and other types of adversity. This book is not meant to be the end-all book on how to face life's challenges. My hope is you will use it as a stepping stone or a piece of the puzzle. If you are facing an incurable disease, your primary source for help or assistance needs to be medical professionals, support groups, and possibly a therapist, which I personally found to be very beneficial. Support groups are a spectacular way for you to stay involved in YOUR battle. This book should complement your primary source for help, not replace it.

As much as I'm glad to share my story with you and I hope you find inspiration in it, I am not a medical doctor. You need to remember this book is just that – my story. Certain chapters may speak to you more than others: integrate those and ditch the rest.

This book was written in hopes of inspiring you to *keep going*. The documentary film *It's Just Parkinson's,* which chronicles my life living with the disease, had the same objective – to educate and inspire.

All my social media accounts, including the website <u>www.itsjustparkinsons.com</u>, were created with the same goal: to spread the IJP mindset and instill hope to those who may feel hopeless. All these platforms were designed to wrap you in a cocoon of inspiration. You win if you never quit.

Make no mistake about it, I am a realist. I'm not here to feed you some rah-rah bullshit. Right now, at this very moment you're reading these words, I am facing the challenge of my lifetime. A battle for my very being. Although I know that ultimately Parkinson's will land the knockout blow, I don't give a damn. I'm going down swinging. I hope you choose to do the same.

John Cullen
Sanibel, Florida
2023

CHAPTER ONE
One in a million

According to the Parkinson's Foundation, nearly one million people in the United States of America have Parkinson's disease and approximately 90,000 Americans are diagnosed with PD each year. Parkinson's is the second-most common neurodegenerative disease after Alzheimer's. I never thought I'd be a Parkinson's statistic.

When you hear the expression "one in a million," it usually describes someone or something special or unique. I don't think I'm either of those things. I see myself as an ordinary guy who has been thrown a curveball in life. I didn't ask to have Parkinson's. I didn't want Parkinson's. I never imagined it would pick me.

I was diagnosed with Parkinson's disease in 2015, yet the news wasn't a complete surprise. I've always been in tune with my body, and in the months leading to my PD diagnosis, I knew something wasn't right. I started experiencing intense random twitching in my right index finger and later in my right leg. I figured it was either

Parkinson's or Multiple Sclerosis (MS) – both medical life-sentences that wreak havoc on the body.

My doctor said most people get upset, feel bewildered and almost always start crying upon learning of their PD diagnosis. I did none of those things. It wasn't that I was numb or in shock, but as mentioned, I knew something was up and had already planned for the worst-case scenario (PD or MS). I had a calm reaction to the official news.

My partner Pattie was the first person I told. She listened intently and was supportive when I discussed my Parkinson's diagnosis. In those early days we rarely discussed my illness in depth, or what living with an incurable disease might mean. Looking back, we were in denial. My PD symptoms were minimal in those early days, and I looked and felt healthy. There were moments when I secretly wondered if it was a mistaken diagnosis.

It took some time before doubt melted away and I grudging-ly accepted my diagnosis was indisputable. I realized I need-ed to pivot and made the conscious decision that I wasn't going to let the disease define or defeat me. I've always been mentally tough, likely the by-product of being the son of a U.S. Marine, so in the early days of my Parkinson's diagnosis I convinced myself I was going to beat it. I truly believed I was going to be the first person in history to conquer this incurable disease. Obviously that didn't happen, and in time my naivete melted away. It was replaced with a strong desire to be positive in the face of my adversity. I came up with the mantra, "It's Just Parkinson's" (IJP).

I clung to IJP like a lifeboat, repeating it to myself whenever I struggled with even minor tasks such as buttoning my shirt or tying my shoelaces. The lifeboat eventually became a lifeline and it helped instil in me a warrior mindset, and in turn I felt inspired, focused, and unstoppable against PD. Although every day Parkinson's takes a part of me I will never get back, I continue to live with this mindset. Don't confuse it with denial. Unlike the early days of my diagnosis, I am fully aware of what Parkinson's is doing to my body and mind, and what it will likely take from me. Yet I choose to be a warrior and to continue fighting – mind over matter. It's a choice I make every day of my life.

Whether during my professional career as a Chief Financial Officer, or during my various athletic pursuits (Spartan racing, marathon running, mountain climbing, etc), I have always faced challenges head-on. In that spirit I've made the conscious choice to face this medical challenge the same way. I truly believe everyone can do this if they have the will and desire. The desire to fight should be irrelevant to the battle's outcome. Knowing the battle will eventually be lost does not mean one shouldn't fight with dignity and grace. Sitting back, giving up, and just wallowing in self-pity while expecting defeat, does nothing to help your body and mind, and is a slippery slope that will likely lead to depression and despair.

What's the point of fighting if you know you're not going to win? For me, it's a matter of dignity and quality of life. The inevitability of reality doesn't deter me from the fight. Yes, I could decide there is no point in fighting Parkinson's and instead crawl into a pit of despair – due to my condition most people wouldn't blame me if I chose this path. But I know that scenario is equivalent to an early death sentence. Instead I choose a more fulfilling life, one with many challenges and struggles, and the daily adventure of dealing with Parkinson's. In my opinion it's still the better choice.

Why do baseball players who are down 10 points in the final inning continue to play with everything they have? I believe the answer is the desire to be your best self regardless of the scenario at hand, or the likely outcome. The hope that those grueling moments will hone body and mind, creating skills to handle the next tough moment.

Along with the desire to live the most fulfilling life possible, I've always enjoyed putting myself in situations where the successful outcome is in doubt. I've always wanted to push myself right to the physical and mental edge, to see how my body and mind react.

It comes from my desire to understand the psyche of people in similar situations. Look at Irish-British polar explorer Sir Ernest Henry Shackleton, whose ship, *Endurance,* became trapped in the Antarctic ice in 1915 and eventually sank, yet incredibly all 27 men under his command survived their grueling ordeal.

Or American cyclist Greg LeMond, who won the Tour de France three times – two of those times were *after* being accidentally shot during a family hunting trip.

Or even American distance swimmer Diana Nyad, who swam from Cuba to Key West, Florida at the age of 64 without the use of a shark cage, after four previous failed attempts. All these amazing individuals excelled even when they faced situations or challenges where the outcome was in doubt. I strive to emulate them and to learn from their examples, by understanding how they handled their challenges from a psychological perspective.

For example, in 2001 at age 42, I decided to run the Milwaukee Marathon for the first time. I had 10 months to get ready for the demanding 26-mile race, which should have been plenty of time to prepare. Normal marathon training involves running hundreds of miles and mentally preparing for the day. The entire 10 months I ran a total of 81 miles, which shouldn't have been adequate preparation. Most runners wouldn't even attempt a marathon with only 81 miles of training, but I was confident I'd finish the race. I had never failed at any athletic challenge.

Surprisingly I wasn't nervous at all when race day came. I figured I'd finish after about four hours. This is key – I didn't allow myself to consider any scenario other than one in which I finished the race, regardless of how long it took. I slipped on my $65 running shoes and sprinted off into the unknown of a marathon. The first 20 miles zoomed along. I reached mile 20 in two hours, twenty-six minutes. The last six miles were grueling, every step was a struggle. But I wanted to test myself in a situation where the outcome was in doubt, so I just tucked in mentally, and attacked. I must be some kind of masochist because I enjoyed the suffering. By the time I finished I had bloody feet. Note to self: don't ever wear cheap shoes, especially to run a marathon! Although it wasn't my intended goal, I missed qualifying for the Boston Marathon by just 25 seconds.

Why am I telling you this story? Because Parkinson's is like a marathon where the outcome is in doubt. All you can do is tuck in mentally and attack. Embrace the challenge and make it about the journey. Just like in a marathon, if you battle your adversity there will be people cheering you on along the way. While the aim is to reach the finish line, that should never be the only goal.

I have many more examples of putting myself in tough situations where the outcome was in doubt. In college, I hitchhiked across the United States – twice. In my 40s, I tackled climbing Mount Rainier in Washington state, even though my only climbing experience was with a ladder. In my 50s, I embarked on a 10-day cycling trip through the Pyrenees mountains – a route normally reserved for the Tour de France. I started powerlifting at age 61 – my deadlift record to date is 470 pounds. Every day I make a conscious effort to face Parkinson's as my latest uncharted challenge.

I thrive in the dark places, those moments when insecurity and self-doubt creep in. Those moments when the voice in my head says, *"Really? You chose this? Well, you've f'd it up this time for sure."* When I hear that voice, I know I've arrived at the dark place and I'd better get going. I'd better get busy to find a way through this morass. I'd better step the f**k up!

To make any situation more manageable, especially ones that seem insurmountable, I first compartmentalize it in my mind. For example, if I have 10 miles left in a marathon, I think of it in three-mile segments. It's no longer a daunting marathon but rather a series of shorter runs, which actually seems doable.

I had never climbed before when I joined a group to summit Mount Rainer in 2011. I left my tent at 2 a.m. The climb to the top and back was estimated to take 15-hours – an astounding undertaking for an amateur climber. Instead of feeling overwhelmed, I visualized the hike in two-hour chunks, and every two hours I would reset my mind to only think about the next two hours of the trek.

Facing my life with Parkinson's disease, I use the same approach:

1. Break it down.
2. Look at the short term.
3. Set seemingly possible short-term goals.
4. Execute.

I accept that not everyone has such an adventurous spirit. For me, hitchhiking in my early 20s helped shape my adult life.

In 1978, when I was 19 years old, I hitchhiked from Ohio to California and back. What was supposed to be a 10-day journey turned into a 15-day odyssey. I ran out of money in Reno, Nevada, and ended up crossing the United States with just a nickel in my pocket! I survived on the kindness of strangers, for which I am forever grateful.

I think hitchhiking helped prepare me for living with PD and those trips helped shape the genius of the IJP mindset. I clearly see parallels between the two. In both scenarios you plan and map out what you hope will happen, but the reality is you can never predict exactly what will happen in the future. When I was hitchhiking, every road trip brought situations or scenarios that had to be dealt with in the moment. The same can be said for everyday life with Parkinson's. Or even regular everyday life: the missed bus, the unexpected phone call, the out-of-stock necessary ingredient at the grocery store.

Every time I opened a car door while hitchhiking, I was stepping into the unknown – the same is true for Parkinson's. While hitchhiking, you may think you know your ultimate destination, but many obstacles or opportunities arise along the way and lead you down a different road – literally. Maybe the driver is only willing to take you to a certain town, and once there you decide to stay. Or during the trip you're told about a new destination you hadn't considered, and suddenly you're changing your itinerary and heading to a new place. The same can be said for Parkinson's disease – each day brings new challenges and hurdles you didn't expect or weren't prepared for. Every day may leave you wondering, *"What I will have to deal with tomorrow?"*

Hitchhiking influenced the direction of my life. I think back on those years with great nostalgia, because out on the open road, anything was possible. I didn't feel life's limitations. I loved the sense of adventure. I was happy to have fate and the kindness of strangers direct my life. I left pieces of myself behind on those journeys; those pieces are still scattered out there, destined to spend eternity on those adventures.

I was between worlds when I hitchhiked. Leaving behind the known, the staid, the predictable, the safe, the unchallenged and the charted. Embracing whatever came my way. Everything I've done since my hitching days has been to re-create that feeling of wanderlust. Whether cycling, running, competing in Spartan obstacle course races, or powerlifting, I've participated in all these activities to re-create the feeling of lust for life and the pure joy of living.

While hitchhiking I also learned one of life's most precious lessons. Out on the open road, I learned how to connect with people. During the many long car rides, I realized that when you meet a stranger who seems different from you, being open and embracing the unfamiliar, truly caring to learn about and connect with another person, is when you realize that in the end, we are more similar than dissimilar.

My battle with Parkinson's is my present-day hitchhiking journey: there is no charted path and I've got to embrace whatever comes. Those of you suffering with this disease may feel alone and that no one can relate to what we are going through, but that's not the case. Whether it's Parkinson's or any other illness or hardship, those who share common ground are bonded with each other. No matter what differences we think we have, in the end we truly are all the same. We're all on a great journey – the journey of life.

This picture was taken in 1978, during my first hitchhiking trip. I'm the one on the left holding the sign, and next to me is my buddy, Frank. We were traveling from Ohio to California, a journey that took us 15 days.

I became addicted to the road during this trip. I left home with just a backpack and $100 in my pocket. I came home a changed man; a true "roads' scholar."

Over the next four years I logged dozens of hitchhiking trips, racking up well over 15,000 miles. I traveled wherever my thumb and the kindness of strangers took me. This was a time long before smartphones or the internet. When we were on the road, we were basically adrift in the vast universe. Each ride was an exercise in being present, and after every trip we returned home profoundly changed.

I purposely never took down anyone's name or contact information because I wanted to live in the moment and not think about the future. Collecting information would've implied a future with the driver, when I didn't intend to have one.

I learned more on the road than I ever learned in any book or classroom. The road was life: a river flowing in every direction. I'd jump into that river and be swept away toward the most unexpected places, at the sheer mercy of the universe.

I met people from all walks of life – there were truck drivers, bus drivers, little old ladies, drug addicts – but mostly they were just regular people. Each ordinary, yet extraordinary in that they momentarily opened their lives to me, a stranger on the side of the road. Those with the least always gave the most.

The road calls to me every now and again but that's a young person's game, and frankly one from a bygone era. But like a siren's song she still calls to me with her promise of adventure. She's wise enough to know I won't join her, but she wants me to know she remembers and misses me. Like a first love, I miss her too.

CHAPTER TWO
You've received life-changing news – now what?

Before I was diagnosed with Parkinson's disease, nothing seemed impossible. I attempted anything that interested me, without giving any thought to the physical limitations. I ran marathons and cycled elite bike routes. I climbed mountains, parasailed, and ran Spartan obstacle course races. Any time I thought about the future it was exciting, and I felt exuberant because nothing seemed out of my reach.

Receiving life-changing news – whether it's a medical diagnosis, the breakup of a marriage, the death of a loved one, or even financial ruin – is devastating. Suddenly and unexpectedly your life is interrupted and changed in ways you never imagined. You may feel scared, confused, and angry. It's OK; all feelings are valid. Your emotions won't be the only thing to double-cross you.

If you've been diagnosed with a debilitating illness like Parkinson's, your body will betray you. There'll be days you don't recognize yourself and doubt your identity. There will also come a time when you have more bad days than good days, and you'll wonder what's the point of living. I am here to tell you life can still be beautiful as long as you choose to fight like hell because you still have more living to do.

Always search for the silver lining. It may be faded and dim but hopefully you can still see it. Even during this dark, difficult, and confusing time, try to be present and appreciate life. While the shock of your new reality may feel overwhelming and all-consuming, a positive attitude is critical in difficult situations. Use an "I got this" attitude. If you don't have an "I got this" attitude, then get one!!

I am aware this isn't an easy task, but please don't let the negative overshadow the beauty that still exists in your life. This kind of thinking is like building a muscle, it's not easy, it takes practice. I've been working on this my whole life: learning to see the silver lining.

Within months of my Parkinson's diagnosis, I noticed many of my abilities began to diminish – some sooner than I was ready for. These days, just getting out of bed feels like a major feat. My walk has become a shuffle – slow, stiff, and rigid. Think of the science fiction monster Frankenstein: that's me. I can no longer perform simple tasks such as buttoning and unbuttoning shirts. Steak knives have become unusable. Putting on socks and shoes is a laborious undertaking. Getting dressed without assistance has become a ridiculous challenge. Rolling over in bed at night is strenuous, if not impossible.

Due to Parkinson's, I can no longer regulate my body temperature, which makes running (and exercising in general) much more difficult. These days, if my body overheats, my mind has trouble coping with this kind of stress and it doesn't know how to handle the situation.

Loss of my executive function has been devastating. I find I can no longer focus, remember instructions, or multitask as I once did. I'm also experiencing high levels of anxiety, and in turn the smallest thing sets me off, and my frustration goes from zero to 100 in seconds. The old me wasn't like this. There are times I don't recognize the man this disease has turned me into. And my friends and family recognize it too.

But over time, I've grown to accept the limitations this disease has bestowed on me. I know this submission may sound unattainable for someone still trying to digest life-changing news. Be gentle and patient with yourself. Try not to get upset about your fate.

You never know what incredible moment might be around the corner. Never blame yourself if you can't do something. Learn to roll with whatever your situation presents. I know it's easier said than done, but a positive attitude is half the battle.

I started experiencing Parkinson's symptoms while riding through the Pyrenees mountains. It turned a challenging goal into a grueling one, struggling for hours cycling uphill in France. But I kept going. I was reduced to counting the white dashes on the road…one pedal at a time. The exhilaration at the top was an incredible moment in my life. I wept with relief that I made it. I never would have had that experience had I given up.

Regardless of what you're experiencing, tell someone. The near future will be challenging so you need to surround yourself with allies – people who will support you through this difficult time. Besides your friends and loved ones, seek out experts and heed their advice.

When you're first diagnosed with Parkinson's disease, your neurologist will assist you in navigating this disorder and help you understand the progression of the disease. They can explain the physical and mental effects of PD and what to expect, such as body stiffness, shaking, anxiety, and loss of executive functions.

The neurologist can also ensure you're taking the proper medications at doses that are right for you. Over time, they can adjust those doses depending on your needs. A neurologist will explain and recommend different types of treatments, such as deep brain stimulation (*DBS*), where electrodes are implanted in the brain to help control motor dysfunction. They can also refer you to your local Parkinson's organization for additional resources.

When I told my neurologist my toes were starting to curl up, which made walking even more difficult, he suggested Botox injections for my calf and foot. The Botox "relaxes" the muscles that are causing my toes to curl. The neurologist can explain the science behind it all. I've had one treatment and so far the results are mixed. My neurologist said it may take a few treatments to see results.

Besides all the vital things a neurologist can do to improve your physical health, equally as important is how they may help your mental health. I personally view my neurologist as my ally and advocate. As such, I keep him in the loop on all things PD. Besides my partner Pattie, he is the first person I speak with about things like depression and the progression of my PD symptoms. Over the years some of my medications stopped being effective and my neurologist adjusted the dose to ensure the meds kept working. Your neurologist is definitely someone you want in your corner!

Regularly consulting and speaking with a therapist will be of great benefit as you navigate this new phase of your life. I'll speak more about my experience with therapy in Chapter Five.

Reach out and engage with local Parkinson's support groups. These groups are invaluable. They offer support for you and your caregiver on this wild journey. They are an excellent resource for just about everything you need to successfully navigate Parkinson's.

When people suddenly face a new hardship, they often get overwhelmed by the uncertainty of the future. Their present gets sidetracked. Up to that point they were living a fulfilling life and were content with their routine. Suddenly they feel scared and saddened and experience feelings of confusion and hopelessness. Without realizing it, they get off the path they were on, and later feel bewildered about how to get back to their old life.

No one can live in yesterday. The old life must become a new life, something equally magical – but different. I am here to prove you can still have a fulfilling life even with Parkinson's, or while battling other adversity. Dare I say you may even experience a *more* fulfilling life, which has been my personal experience so far.

It's important not to think of Parkinson's, or whatever adversity you face, as a life sentence. While PD is currently incurable, I am still in control of my life's narrative. I've taken up powerlifting. I've written this book. Who knows what adventure awaits? I face Parkinson's head-on and fight it with everything I have. It's my personal battle and I see myself as a warrior. I have Parkinson's, but Parkinson's doesn't have me.

CHAPTER THREE
How to move forward when your future is in doubt

One of life's greatest riddles is how to live a worthwhile life, despite adversity. How does one have a fulfilling existence no matter the obstacles they face?

The obstacle in my life is Parkinson's disease, but everyone, at some point in their life, will face their own challenge or difficulty. Whether it's a medical illness, or a professional hurdle, a financial burden, or a complicated relationship–regardless of the adversity or hardship life may hand us, we need to remember we have control over how we react to it.

Even when life's hardships seem impossible to escape, you still have a choice regarding how you deal with them. Don't crawl into a hole because you have Parkinson's disease, or any other illness or ailment. Don't give up when you're going through a divorce, job loss, or even bankruptcy. Regardless of what challenges you're facing, and there may be many factors that could potentially derail you from a life well-lived, strive to move forward in a meaningful way. Make the conscious decision that you want to have a worthwhile existence. The first step to moving forward is positivity. If you keep thinking negatively, and have the attitude that everything is impossible, chances are you won't succeed.

When I was much younger, I remember being in a baseball game and not having a positive attitude. Somehow, I knew before I stepped into the batter's box that I was going to strike out. And guess what? I did. If only I knew then what I know now about having a positive attitude.

If you program your mind to believe whatever you strive for is attainable, there is a high probability of success. I have made the conscious decision to be positive about my illness and not let Parkinson's define me.

Not letting something define you doesn't mean you won't emerge changed by it. All major life experiences mold us in one way or another; sometimes it's obvious, other times it's subtle. Change is inevitable and it's important to embrace it on your own terms. I've worked very hard to avoid letting Parkinson's define me. That doesn't mean it hasn't changed me, because it *has* changed me and probably for the better. The important distinction is I choose to be in the driver's seat of my life's journey. We all have this choice; we just need to be brave enough to believe it.

When you're diagnosed with Parkinson's disease it's a devastating blow to your reality. You need to quickly find a way to deal with it and to cope with the trauma, otherwise you run the risk of slipping into major hopelessness or even a deep depression.

When I was first diagnosed with Parkinson's, I convinced myself I was going to beat the disease. I thought I would be the first person in the world to overcome this incurable disease. Obviously, that didn't happen. When that realization struck me, I was emotionally unfazed. Instead, I became even more determined to fight with all my might.

Every day Parkinson's takes a part of me I will never get back. To cope, I created a mantra to help me deal with, and accept my life changes. That mantra is: "It's Just Parkinson's" (IJP).

It may shock some people to hear someone suffering from a debilitating and life-changing disease say, *"It's Just Parkinson's."* Don't make the mistake of thinking I am in denial about the disease, or that I have an aloof attitude about the seriousness of my illness. When I say, *"It's Just Parkinson's,"* it means a few things. For starters, it's my way of cutting this terrible disease down to size. Trust me, I know having Parkinson's is a big deal, I just don't need to be reminded of that fact every second of the day. Instead of saying, *"Oh my god, I've got Parkinson's,"* I say, *"It's Just Parkinson's. I got this!"*

I was recently running in the woods when my legs gave out and I fell flat on my face. I could have just limped back home. IJP got me up and I continued that run with serious determination.

My saying, "It's Just Parkinson's" gives *me* the power and strips it away from the disease, so Parkinson's has less prominence in my life. My life is also about my partner Pattie, powerlifting, and trying new pursuits. Parkinson's is just one aspect—it's not my whole life.

Parkinson's doesn't determine how I live my life, I determine that. Finally, I use the phrase to help empower others facing a significant challenge in their lives. When they hear me say IJP, they see how I've cut this thing down to size. They see how I've taken the power *from* Parkinson's, which in turn empowers them to face their challenges.

Although the phrase "It's Just Parkinson's," IJP includes the word "Parkinson's," IJP has evolved into something much broader. IJP has become a movement I hope people from all walks of life embrace.

IJP provides a platform for those facing a challenge in their life. Its underlying themes nurture people as they navigate through their difficulties. Themes such as ROCK–LIGHT—HOPE provide people with support to face and defeat their challenges. IJP's mission is simple: to be the rock for those facing a battle, to provide light for those lost in the dark, and to give hope to those who feel defeated. ROCK–LIGHT–HOPE.

A concept encased in the IJP worldview is IJP mindset. I distinguish it as a warrior attitude fostered by the IJP themes of ROCK–LIGHT–HOPE. IJP mindset is defined as the established set of attitudes held by someone. This means you have the choice whether you want to live a fulfilling life or not. You may think Parkinson's (or whatever ails you) has taken away your freedom to make your own decisions, but this is not completely true. You can still choose how you want to live your life, what kind of quality of life you want to have, and how you want to face your adversity.

Many people have adopted the IJP mindset. Fred, 72, in Fort Myers, Florida had given up his fight against Parkinson's and was basically confined to his couch all day. He learned about the IJP mindset and decided to get back into the fight. He's now exercising regularly by walking around his neighborhood. The power of IJP is incredible.

My hope is the IJP mantra will serve as a reminder to never give up, to stay positive, and never, ever surrender. Despite your challenges, with the right mindset, you have the opportunity to live a purposeful life.

Physical activity has always been extremely important to me, and I have been athletic my whole life. When I returned home from the Pyrenees cycling trip, I realized I could no longer ride a bicycle safely (a beloved activity since my teenage years). My reaction time became so slow I could no longer control the bicycle at high speeds, especially traveling downhill. Take time to grieve a loss like this in your life, but then look around—there are dozens of other activities waiting for you to try.

Of course, I mourned the loss of my cycling ability. It was tremendously difficult to give up cycling. I chose to give away all my cycling equipment, including my prized top-of-the-line racing bike which was only two years old. As my friend drove off with my bike in his trunk, I felt a great sense of loss. It was gutting.

It would have been easy to feel depressed and defeated that I could no longer bicycle, and no one would have blamed me for feeling this way. I chose not to let myself fall into that trap, and instead focused on finding new activities to explore, such as Spartan obstacle course races and powerlifting.

To my great surprise, once I accepted the changes to my lifestyle, I realized the situation was not as dire as I thought, and ironically my life was more enriched because I was forced to try new things.

Sometimes in life we're so focused on the hurt and sadness caused by certain doors closing, we miss seeing that windows to new opportunities and adventures may be opening.

When it comes to life-altering illnesses, change doesn't usually happen overnight. Parkinson's is an incremental disease which means change happens slowly. I didn't just wake up one day no longer able to ride a bike, it happened gradually over two years. I went from riding elite bike routes, such as portions of the Tour de France race course, to only cycling five miles at a time, to no longer being able to ride at all.

Same goes for running. I loved running and for many years (the "running phase" of my life) I'd commute to work by running. I'd run seven miles a day, but over the years my running has been compromised by the effect Parkinson's has on my gait. Now, I can barely run at all. Instead, I have started jogging, but I know one day I won't be able to do that either.

Change is difficult and sometimes we're faced with circumstances that feel overwhelming. Whatever hurdle comes your way I hope the IJP mindset inspires and brings you hope. Whether it's something major such as a health issue (as in my case), the breakdown of a relationship, stress at work, financial woes, or even dealing with a difficult person, no matter the issue (big or small), my hope is that people turn to and find inspiration and comfort in the IJP ethos. When life gets you down (and it will), I hope you tap into the IJP mindset and let it be your rock, and a beacon of light you can steer toward no matter the storm you're facing.

For me, it's during the most difficult moments in my life when I rely on the IJP spirit. When I participated in Spartan races, which are grueling 6 and 13-mile obstacle course races, I found myself relying on my IJP spirit–a true warrior attitude–to pull me through to the finish line. At the beginning of the race I'm fresh and ready to go. As the race progresses, I become fatigued and my PD symptoms overwhelm me. I just repeat, "Keep going John, do not quit." Keep. Going. Every single step gets me closer to the finish line.

The honest recognition of one's current circumstances, and the identification and elimination of obstacles, is what allows us to live our best life. Elimination of an obstacle doesn't necessarily mean that obstacle is destroyed; it simply means the obstacle no longer impedes one from living their best life. IJP mindset is the long-term application of inspiration and focus to help overcome obstacles in your life. Passion and persistence—these elements will provide you with the grit to be unstoppable.

Inspiration and passion are critically important. You can't step up to a challenge if you're not inspired to do so. Facing a challenge without inspiration will certainly result in failure. Some people call it being fired up, or impassioned, or even excited. Whatever you call it, it's essential to your success. For me, every obstacle I've successfully overcome started with inspiration, whether it was hitchhiking from one end of the country to the other, or chasing a promotion.

Certain obstacles, like Parkinson's, require daily focus, or at best, they must be addressed and monitored regularly. Without single-minded focus and persistence, you'll most likely be doomed to failure. I equate focus and persistence to climbing a mountain—it may look daunting, but you just take it one step at a time. There's no shortcut. Put one foot in front of the other and eventually you'll get there. One step at a time until you reach the summit. There's no easy way to the top. You must focus on the long-term goal and the desired outcome. Inspiration and focus form the foundation of grit, and grit is what gets stuff done. I have faith in you.

CHAPTER FOUR
Acknowledge and embrace change

It's important to acknowledge your life has changed–forever. There is the before, and the after. You are in the after. Just like how we can't return to being 10 years old again, there is no way to return to the before—not with Parkinson's.

But more than just recognizing your life has changed, it's important to also mourn the loss of your old life. It's OK to feel your journey has taken an unwelcome turn. Heed the hurt and the pain. Do not bottle up these feelings or "put on a brave face." You're entitled to feel sad, at least temporarily.

I spent years cycling all over the world, which made it tremendously difficult for me to give up bicycling when I could no longer ride safely. I was devastated. I grieved and wept as if I had lost a member of my own family.

Crying is cathartic. If you just bury these feelings and pretend you're not bothered by the sudden life changes, these feelings will likely come back in a more serious manner.

Like any grieving, if you don't address the root cause of the trauma early on, it may morph into a bigger issue, such as depression, which can be much harder to address down the road.

It was extremely upsetting when I started having difficulty riding my bike. I first noticed something was wrong in 2014. I was 55, on a bike tour, and we were riding in the French Pyrenees mountains. I'd been dreaming of this trip for several years and I was excited to be checking it off my bucket list. We rode our bikes 80 miles a day, 40 miles of climbing and 40 miles of descending, every day for eight days. Part of the tour was the same route used during the Tour de France, which was thrilling. But on my first ride I noticed my right leg was not keeping up. I couldn't get it to do the things the left leg could do. My right leg felt weaker and uncoordinated. Even though I was strapped into the bike pedals, I could tell the right leg wasn't producing the same power as the left. Out of a group of 13 cyclists, I came in last every single day by at least an hour. I was alarmed and panicked at the prospect of something being physically wrong with me.

Within 24 months of that trip, I could no longer safely ride a bike. Yet I couldn't just walk away from 30 years of cycling and not be devastated. To this day, I cannot look at a bicycle without being transported back to a time when I could ride.

More than just being heartbroken by the loss of an activity I loved, not being able to cycle as I once did was a sign my Parkinson's was progressing, and I was starting to realize what was to come. As my body started betraying me and tremors crept in, I was suddenly dragging my feet, and simple daily tasks like getting dressed started becoming difficult. I'm not a good enough actor to pretend I wasn't bothered by what was transpiring, and instead I mourned the loss of my past independent life.

After about five years of having Parkinson's, the totality of the independent life I had lost really struck me. On a few occasions I got so upset I just lost it. A handful of times I broke down and had a meltdown: crying, or more accurately wailing, begging my disease not to take me. Many nights in despair I prayed to the universe, pleading, "*Please stop. I don't want to go this way; I want my old self back.*" The silence was deafening.

Luckily, I had a therapist who helped me process the emotions I was feeling. My therapist guided me through that transitional period and reassured me it was OK and necessary to mourn such losses, because they *are* losses. I was encouraged to release the pain, through tears or otherwise, without feeling shame for needing the catharsis.

At the end of the day, I know this disease will ultimately win, but I choose to battle against it. The reality doesn't deter me from the fight ahead. I won't stop fighting. Many people may argue, "*What's the point if you know you aren't going to win?*" It goes back to quality of life. Sure, you can say, "What's the point?" and crawl into a pit of despair and never come out, but that's basically choosing to end your life while technically still living. The choice is yours to decide which scenario will make your life more fulfilling.

I have always been driven—I would rather go down fighting than passively accept my fate. But for anyone: it's never too late to live, to learn, to experience new things, no matter what you're facing. Quality of life is key.

Where does positive thinking end and reality kick in? That's a valid question. From my experience, I've come to realize there is great power in being an optimist. Please don't associate positive thinking in the face of a difficult situation, or even in the face of certain defeat, with being delusional. I believe positivity equals hope, and as they say, hope dies last.

If you're having a hard time being positive about your current, or future situation, it may help to ask yourself what makes a "regular" life a well-lived life? I think a lot of people facing adversity get stuck on the idea their situation is holding them back, or not allowing them to live the best life possible. Unfortunately, for some people this may be true, there is no sugarcoating that. Yet some people use their hardship as an excuse, and the negativity is needless.

It's important to be realistic about what the trajectory of your life likely would've been, even if you weren't faced with adversity. Don't judge your current situation by unattainable standards that wouldn't be possible even if you didn't have adversity in your life. I'm currently 64 years old and I can't do some of the things I did when I was 18 years old. That's my reality and I can't blame Parkinson's for it.

Let's say you're someone who was recently in a car accident and became disabled. As a result, your mobility was affected and you now use a wheelchair to get around. If before your accident you were afraid of heights and didn't enjoy being in nature, why after your accident are you upset that you can't go hiking or mountain climbing? This example may seem extreme, but the sentiment is real. It's ridiculous to be distressed about something you didn't want in the first place, and yet people facing adversity seem to fall into this trap regularly.

Luckily I didn't fall into this trap because I'm honest with myself about my abilities and what I would or wouldn't have tried before Parkinson's. I don't lament not being able to pilot a plane because I was never interested in flying one.

I understand wanting to blame your adversity for the fact your life has changed or is changing, but you need to be realistic about what your life would've been like even without your current situation. It's a cop-out to automatically blame our adversity for everything. Yes, we may face an extra life hurdle (heck more than just one, maybe a dozen), but we can't and shouldn't blame anything and everything on our hardship. We can't be upset that life isn't giving us a clean slate when under "regular" circumstances we wouldn't have a clean slate anyway.

A life well lived is a life with purpose, and that may include many things, such as: family, friends, and experiences. Despite the hurdles I face, I make a conscious effort to enrich my life by surrounding myself with people I love and doing things that make me happy. My friends, family, and the people I've met along the way, all provide a sense of connectivity.

I'm also still very curious about the world, and every chance I get I try new activities or hobbies. I've always enjoyed physical activity and being outdoors, so I continue to seek out such experiences.

Parkinson's has taken away my ability to do some of the things I love, but as a result I've pivoted. Instead of cycling and running, I now powerlift and go walking. I recently tried fishing and loved it! I'm not good at baiting hooks but I can reel them in. That experience taught me there are still new and exciting adventures in my life, even after my Parkinson's diagnosis. Life doesn't end because you've been handed a hardship. There may be many wonderful moments waiting for you, as long as you're open to trying something new.

Purpose may also mean being a good friend, a good neighbor, a good spouse/parent/child, etc. You don't have to climb Mount Everest or achieve a superhuman task to have purpose in your life. There is value in the everyday moments. Everyday adventures may range from hanging out with friends, seeing a movie, going for a walk, or going to a restaurant for dinner. Special moments can be found in the ordinary, and the ordinary may easily become extraordinary. Lean into these moments and embrace them.

CHAPTER FIVE
Depression—it may be more than just feeling sad

How do you move forward when your future is in doubt? How do you keep hope alive when the outcome appears bleak? Why get up every day and fight when you know it'll be a losing battle? The answers to all these questions are the same: GRIT.

Grit is a trait possessed by individuals who demonstrate passion and perseverance toward a goal despite being confronted by significant obstacles and distractions. Regardless of the adversity you face, attack it and overcome it with grit.

If you don't transition to a positive mindset, that's when depression may kick in, and there's a good chance that fighting depression will be a harder battle than whatever hardship you're already facing.

Sometimes depression isn't simply about being sad. For those like me who've been diagnosed with Parkinson's disease, you may be affected by a chemical imbalance due to the lack of dopamine in your body. Dopamine is a neurotransmitter made in your brain which acts as a chemical messenger communicating between the nerve cells in your brain and the rest of your body. It is known as the "feel-good" hormone because it gives you a sense of pleasure. High or low levels of dopamine are associated with several mental health and neurological diseases. People with PD have a lack of dopamine in their body, and as a result they often experience depression.

Dopamine levels can be recharged by taking medication prescribed by your doctor, and there are also other ways to naturally boost or replenish dopamine. Getting sufficient sleep, exercising, eating protein, taking probiotics and vitamins, listening to music, meditating, and spending time in the sun, can all boost dopamine levels. Overall, a balanced diet and lifestyle are essential to increasing your body's natural production of dopamine and helping diminish the risk of depression.

Whatever the cause of your depression, never feel ashamed of how you're feeling. Although I've tried to be open and honest about my Parkinson's battle, there is one crucial part of my journey I haven't openly discussed until now.

I've suffered from bouts of depression over the years. Initially, feelings of depression presented themselves periodically, from age 40 to 55. In the period leading up to my Parkinson's diagnosis, my spells of depression were more frequent and sometimes intense. I now know that frequent periods of depression can be a precursor to a Parkinson's diagnosis. The sad feelings would come out of nowhere and blindside me. Sometimes those low feelings would really have me struggling. At times I was so deeply depressed the thought of suicide would briefly cross my mind.

If this happens to you and thoughts of suicide persist, it's a red flag and you need to seek help immediately. Talk to your doctor about your medication, and call your therapist for support and to review strategies. Through this process I learned I'm not alone and I have a team of people to call on for help.

One of the scariest moments happened on arguably one of the best days of my life. I was 62 and five years into my Parkinson's diagnosis. I had just competed in a powerlifting competition and was feeling so empowered—I was breaking the mold of what someone with Parkinson's could achieve. By stressing my central nervous system through powerlifting, I was pushing back against PD, and I felt reborn.

That feeling didn't last long. Ironically, I went from feeling the extreme high of having people cheering me on and telling me how inspiring I was, to feeling completely hopeless. No one I met that day would ever imagine that only hours later I would be plagued by suicidal thoughts.

This time it wasn't an emotional depression, but a chemical one. By giving my all at the powerlifting competition I essentially overstressed my body, and in the process, I depleted my dopamine levels. The competition itself was fantastic and incredibly stimulating, from the announcer to the music pumping, to the crowds cheering me on. I met so many people that day who asked about my Parkinson's and felt a real sense of kinship with all the competitors. We truly supported each other. But after the competition was over, on my way home, I went from feeling euphoric to feeling completely empty. The change in my mood was quick and dangerous. Almost immediately suicidal thoughts engulfed me, and I felt coerced to act upon them. Unfortunately, I wasn't taking antidepressants at the time, which is how the situation got so dire—I only started taking antidepressants six years after my PD diagnosis. Fortunately, I reached out for help and made a phone call that saved my life.

This is no joke. If you're entertaining any thoughts of harming yourself, immediately reach out to your support network. If that's not possible contact a suicide prevention line.

If you live or are based in the United States and are contemplating suicide, or are in emotional distress, I encourage you to call the Suicide & Crisis Lifeline by simply dialing 9-8-8 from your phone. You'll be immediately connected with a network of over 200 crisis centers. This service is available 24/7 and is free to access.

While a healthy body and mind are a big part of the equation, I now know positivity isn't enough to combat depression. These days, I am on antidepressants my doctor prescribed, and feelings of depression or suicidal thoughts are generally gone. The medication counterbalances the loss of dopamine and I don't feel sad on a regular basis. My prescribed antidepressants help my mood, and about once a year my doctor adjusts my meds to ensure they continue working for me.

I highly recommend immediately discussing medication options with your doctor, once you're diagnosed with any debilitating disease, or if you're feeling overwhelming sadness due to your current situation. Don't wait for the sadness to creep in like I did. Most likely your physician will want to discuss these options with you as soon as possible.

As I mentioned earlier, depression can be a precursor to Parkinson's and I suffered from depression throughout my life. But at the time, I didn't want to be on medication. After my Parkinson's diagnosis, my initial PD drug load was aimed at mobility issues rather than cognitive issues. As a result, it wasn't until several years after my diagnosis that I confronted my depression. During that time I fought hard against the depression, but without the help of antidepressants it was a losing battle, since every day my brain was being depleted of more and more dopamine. Antidepressants quite literally saved my life.

Even if you think you don't need antidepressants right away, I still recommend discussing the matter with your doctor. That way, when the time comes that you need them, you won't be scrambling, and you'll be better equipped to address any mood swings or feelings of sadness. I suffered in silence for a long time thinking I could beat it on my own. But you don't have to.

It's not easy for me to discuss the moments in my life when I was so depressed I contemplated suicide. I'm not embarrassed, because I know they were the result of extreme side effects caused by my disease, and a result of the loss of dopamine in my brain, but I don't like to dwell on those memories. I know those moments don't define me and thankfully those occasions have been few and far between. The reason I'm sharing this very personal part of my Parkinson's journey with you is so that if you're experiencing something similar, I want you to know you are not alone, and you shouldn't feel ashamed. Experiencing depression isn't about being "strong" or "weak," and we shouldn't feel ashamed about it.

People with chronic illness often struggle with depression, worry, anger, and anxiety. As a result of my Parkinson's disease, I too have been inflicted with these side effects and disorders. I've found antidepressants alone aren't enough. A crucial part of my emotional rehabilitation has resulted from speaking with a therapist. My therapist explained medication alone usually only improves 50 percent of feelings of sadness or chronic depression, so therapy needs to be included for improved mental health.

I've been seeing a therapist on and off for about about fifteen years. Initially, in my 40s, I went to therapy to help me better understand the dynamics surrounding key relationships. Later, I consulted my therapist as I went through my divorce. Most recently, I've been seeing my therapist to work through my Parkinson's diagnosis.

I've had the same therapist since the beginning. I was lucky to have found someone I felt comfortable confiding in, and whose advice and insights I found beneficial. Having a continuous therapist-client relationship means the advice I receive is consistent. I don't need to start over with a new, unproven therapist each time. And she knows me well. She has reinforced to me that I have the power to change my life and face adversity on my terms.

Like most relationships, you need to make sure you're comfortable with the person you are confiding in, so if you need to try a few different therapists before you find one who you connect with, that's OK. Don't be disheartened if you don't find the right therapist immediately. Don't give up! Ask friends, family members and others you know if they'll briefly talk about their therapist, and one of them may sound like the right fit for you.

I currently speak with my therapist every two weeks, but in the beginning we met weekly. Some people may need more time with a therapist, others will need less. Don't focus on what others are doing: find a system that works for you and your mental health needs.

Therapy is like any other remedial treatment. I see no difference between going to a therapist to discuss issues or concerns in my life, with going to a physical therapist to treat an injury like a sprained ankle. Both professions exist to help us be healthy. Physical health should not be prioritized over mental health—we need both to be our best selves.

It is scary knowing that even while I'm trying to live my life with positivity, the chemicals and hormones in my body (specifically dopamine) may affect my mood in very serious ways. Having a healthy lifestyle, taking my prescribed medication, speaking with a therapist, and having a warrior mindset, are how I continue battling depression. It's a powerful reminder to myself—and a very important lesson I wanted to share.

CHAPTER SIX
You are not alone

There are more than 10 million people in the world living with Parkinson's disease, according to parkinsons.org. If, like me, you're one of those people, welcome to a very big club. I'm sorry this is happening to you, but thankfully there are tools and a community to help you.

It's natural to have moments when you feel you're traveling down a solitary path, but I'm here to remind you this isn't the case. Those of us living with Parkinson's have much more than just the disease in common; we can relate to each other, and we understand the physical and mental toll it takes on us. You don't need to fight this battle by yourself —there are allies willing and eager to support you in your time of need, whether for doctor referrals or for support groups. My advice is to look up your local Parkinson's chapter and contact them directly.

There are countless communities and groups experiencing exactly what you're going through. These groups were formed with the very purpose of offering support and advice to people just like you and me. It's time to stop throwing yourself a pity party, because there are literally millions of other people just like you.

For those of us struggling with something (whether an illness or another difficult life situation), our battle bonds us and we are automatically connected. I genuinely feel I am on the same team as others battling adversity, and I see our shared struggles as a group effort. Like any team we must lift each other up. When I'm down others need to lift me up, and when I'm up I'll help lift others. A group of people is almost always stronger than an individual, hence the expression: *strength in numbers.*

My dad was a U.S. Marine so I often think of the military phrase: *carry the wounded.* It applies to people in everyday life who're battling adversity; we need to always carry each other. (The entire phrase is: *Carry the wounded and shoot the stragglers.* So whatever you do, don't straggle!!)

There are countless support groups available for whatever adversity you are experiencing. If, like me, you have Parkinson's disease, I encourage you to reach out to PD support organizations for help.

I confess that early in my Parkinson's journey I wasn't interested in meeting or speaking with anyone else who suffered from the disease. I shunned any Parkinson's support groups or communities because I mistakenly thought my journey was unique and I didn't want to be influenced by other people's experiences.

It took me five years to finally reach out to the Parkinson's community. I'm so glad I did, because I met people in the same situation I'm in. I wish I'd reached out sooner; I could've avoided feeling so alone in my struggle.

It took until I created the IJP mindset (the honest recognition of one's current circumstances and the identification and elimination of obstacles impeding someone from living their best life), and I began sharing that message online and through the documentary film, *It's Just Parkinson's,* to realize I inadvertently invented my own support group. The irony is not lost on me. Life sure is funny sometimes, huh?

Now that I'm older (and wiser), I encourage you to join a support group for the many useful resources, and to help navigate whatever hardship you're experiencing. If you're someone who has Parkinson's disease, there are local groups in almost every city. If there isn't one in your area, you can find countless websites like parkinsons.org, allowing you to directly connect with other PD sufferers.

Besides online resources, you can access books on just about every topic, as well as podcasts, which are one of my new favourite resources. The podcasts range from how to live independently with Parkinson's, to exercise, to even a Parkinson's playlist!

Be open to meeting people who can help you on your journey; the resources exist, you just need to seek them out. If you're not quite ready to speak about your adversity with strangers, maybe start with the people around you, such as your family and friends. I know it can be difficult to open up to others and let them in when we're hurting, but I hope you do just that. Life is hard so don't be afraid to lean on others. Chances are the people in your life or your community want to help you–their support is a gift, accept it graciously. If the situation was reversed, wouldn't you want your friend or neighbor to accept your support? Giving to others is a gift and we need to allow others the opportunity to have this gift.

Asking and allowing people to support or comfort you is a bonding experience which provides mutual benefits to both parties. I'm constantly asking people at the gym to help me with things like buttoning my shirt or tying my shoes, and I feel the experience has brought me closer to these individuals. Even during grueling Spartan obstacle course races, when I mentioned I had Parkinson's to a fellow competitor, they invariably assisted and stayed with me along the course.

Most people take pride in being useful and may feel honored to be asked for their assistance. Who doesn't feel good after helping someone else? At home, I can spend 45 minutes getting dressed every morning, or I can ask my caregiver Pattie for help. I always choose the latter and I believe it's added another layer of intimacy and affection to our relationship.

By sharing your experience and asking others for help, they're likely to feel useful and part of the solution, thus making them an ally that you absolutely need during this time in your life.

Some caregivers may view helping someone get dressed as just one more thing they have to do. Over time, these feelings can turn into anger, frustration, and resentment. I get it. As time goes by, the caregiver's load increases as the Parkinson's patient becomes more dependent. As I lose my abilities, I'm thankful to have a caregiver who assists me in everything from toweling me after a shower to cutting up my food.

It's also important for caregivers to seek support. Most Parkinson's organizations have a community to help the caregiver. It's important to remember while you're trying to navigate this difficult time in your life, you aren't the only one. Whatever you're experiencing is impacting your family and loved ones. While this isn't happening directly to them, they aren't immune to the side effects of the situation.

Your loved ones may be feeling awkward or uncomfortable, especially if you're shutting them out of your life and not confiding in them about how you're feeling. I understand not wanting to burden them with what you're experiencing, but whether you realize it or not, they too are part of this journey and this is hard on them. Open up to them, be vulnerable, don't be scared to tell them exactly how you're feeling. They're probably stronger than you think. Being honest with them helps them understand what you're going through, and, in the process, they may better help you navigate these uncharted waters.

For some people (like myself), we don't just need emotional support, we also need part-time or full-time caregivers to help us in our everyday life. I couldn't get through the day without assistance from my loving partner Pattie. I rely on her for many things I can no longer do alone—it's a special person who'll pull up your underwear for you every day!

If you're someone who requires a personal support worker, or a family member has taken on that role, be aware of what they're going through and what their needs might be. Besides their love for you, they in turn, due to their sheer proximity to you, are being transformed by what you're going through, and may be feeling stressed and overwhelmed.

If you're angry about your situation, chances are your caregiver also feels a degree of animosity or frustration. It's not uncommon for a caregiver to feel bitter or upset. This is natural and you shouldn't blame them for feeling this way. They've suddenly been parachuted into a very difficult situation they didn't ask to be in. If you have moments when you're angry and want to shout, *"WHY ME?"* then imagine how your caregiver may feel.

It's completely understandable for a caregiver to get frustrated or angry for picking up the slack when the person they're caring for has given up on life and doesn't want to do anything for themselves. If suddenly the caregiver is doing everything, and the patient isn't contributing in any way, this isn't fair, and as a result they may feel resentful. This is a completely valid and human reaction and they shouldn't be demonized if they confess to such feelings.

Of course, there are individuals not physically capable of doing certain things due to their illness, and as such the burden *will* fall on their caregiver. If this is your reality, be supportive of your supporters. Don't feel entitled to their love and care. They aren't obligated to be part of your journey. There will be times where one or both of you will be frustrated. Step back and take a deep breath. They're here because they want to help you. In turn, you must acknowledge their efforts. Be optimistic, have a positive attitude, acknowledge their help, and show them gratitude. You're fortunate to have loved ones and caregivers with you on every step of this journey—never take them for granted.

Attitude is a BIG factor in this game. Have a positive attitude! Don't turn toxic just because you're having a bad day. Don't spew negativity into the situation. Remember the adage: "If you can't say something nice…" Hello? This applies to you. Close your mouth and don't complain. Yes, we're in this together but we don't need to listen to you whine. There's no place for a toxic, non-productive situation.

2012. After climbing nothing more than a ladder all my life, I decided to climb and summit Mount Rainier in Washington State. Here we are on our way to the summit. We were roped in for safety.

1990-2018. I've competed in well over 200 bicycle and foot races in my lifetime. I kept every number for every race. Here are a few of them. Each one represents an epic battle fought and won.

2013. One of my bucket list items was to bicycle the entire length of the Skyline Drive / Blue Ridge Parkway in the USA. The total length of the ride was just short of 600 miles. With a total elevation gain of 65,000 feet. Here I am posing with my riding partner at the highest point on the ride.

2014. Another bucket list item was to bicycle through the Pyrenees mountains in France. It was an 8-day ride covering 75 miles and 10,000 feet of climbing every day. It was on this ride that I discovered my right leg could not keep up with my left leg. This was the start of my Parkinson's journey.

2017. During most races, I ran alone. Not good enough to hang with the elite runners yet faster than the average runner. I consistently finished in the top 10%.

2018. I ran a number of Spartan races from 2017-2019. Due to Parkinson's effects on me, I was never certain that I would finish a race I started. During the race my dopamine levels would crash. My body would freeze up and I would struggle through to the finish line. I finished every race I started.

2018. Before there was "IJP" there was "Find a way". This was the mantra that Diana Nyad used to compel her to complete her epic swim from Cuba to Florida. I adopted her mantra and used it to carry me through Spartan obstacle course races. During those races, I would encounter times I wasn't sure I'd finish. I would call out, "Find a way John! Find a way to finish the race." It was as if Diana was right beside me. Urging me on. Carrying me to the finish. She became my all time hero. I met her in 2018 and vowed to tell her what she meant to me. Unfortunately, my emotions overwhelmed me and I spent the entirety of our meeting bawling my eyes out.

2020. I found that powerlifting helped ease my Parkinson's symptoms. With this lift, I broke my personal record and lifted 525 pounds. Not bad for 62 years old.

2021. As part of the release of the documentary *It's Just Parkinson's* we held a red-carpet premiere. Here Pattie and I greet our 200 guests. It was a spectacular evening. I was overwhelmed at the response to our film. It's a good thing we handed out tissues!

2021. Members of the production team of *It's Just Parkinson's* at the red-carpet premiere. From left: Director of Photography Thomas C. Webb, Producer/Director Diane Akam, Story Producer & Writer Mary Dartis, myself, Pattie, Post Production Supervisor & Editor Julian Francis Adderley, and Composer Julien Verschooris.

2022. Since the release of our documentary *It's Just Parkinson's*, we've had the good fortune to personally show it to a variety of groups. Here we are hosting a showing in Fort Myers, Florida.

2022. IJP has an extensive following and support. Here I am posing with Pattie and two of our biggest supporters: Angie and Joe McGilvrey of Apex Physical Therapy in Fort Myers, Florida.

2023. IJP has brought a variety of people from all walks of life into my life. Ivan Suãrez is a great example. He and I come from completely different backgrounds and on that account alone you'd think our partnership would not work. Yet our alliance works well. From the very beginning Ivan has supported and helped IJP grow from a concept to a budding internationally recognized name brand.

CHAPTER SEVEN
Own your adversity

There is great power in owning your adversity. Let people know what's going on in your life. Tell everyone who will listen. Although at present you may not have control over certain aspects of your life, you have absolute control over how you address your situation. By acknowledging the challenges you're currently facing, you'll likely gain a newfound sense of freedom during an otherwise difficult time.

I encourage people with Parkinson's to not hide their diagnosis. Tell everyone you have PD and don't be ashamed of it. This takes the stigma out of it. If you appear comfortable discussing your disease, people in turn will be comfortable asking you questions, and will likely educate themselves in the process. Encourage a dialogue. Whether you want to or not, you are now a Parkinson's ambassador—take up the mantle with pride.

If it's not an illness you're battling, discuss whatever troubles you. If you're depressed and contemplating suicide, seek help. If you're having financial struggles, consider a credit counseling service. If you're having a difficult relationship with someone, look for ways to mediate the situation. Whatever is upsetting you, tell someone and find individuals or organizations that offer support.

Besides the autonomy that comes with owning your adversity, you're also destigmatizing your hardship. Often people who are going through a tough time (whether it's an illness or another issue) feel ashamed about their predicament. Although it's human to sometimes feel embarrassed about your adversity and avoid telling people about what you're experiencing, strive to take your illness or hardship out of the shadows. Not feeling embarrassed about your hardship equates to not feeling alone, and there is a straight line between feeling ashamed about a situation and feeling isolated by it.

I personally never felt embarrassed about my Parkinson's diagnosis, although in the beginning I was in denial. I did tell people immediately. A lot of people's first reaction was, *"Oh, that's too bad."* I appreciated their empathy but quickly realized most people were unfamiliar with the disease and didn't know how to react because they didn't know what PD was or how it would affect my life. I now realize that in the process of informing my friends, family, and the public, I was also educating them about Parkinson's disease. The lesson this taught me was that whether we realize it or not, we are ambassadors for whatever adversity we're experiencing, and we have the choice whether we make that a positive or negative experience.

Taking control of how we disclose our hardship and injecting some humor, helps a great deal. When I see people looking at me quizzically, I know they're wondering what is different about me. By choosing to inform and educate them about my disease, that's my way of recovering control over my life. It's how I reclaim my power and own my existence. In such instances I often say to people, "*If it looks as though I have Parkinson's, it's because I do.*" In most cases once people know about my PD, they're more comfortable and relaxed around me, as opposed to before I told them.

I remember one occasion when I was going through security at Wisconsin's Milwaukee airport. I was feeling particularly rigid that day, and as a result I was moving super slowly. I noticed a security guard watching me from afar. He eventually approached me and asked if I was OK. I responded with, "*I'm not drunk, I have Parkinson's.*" We both laughed and the tension was eased.

Recently, I was at a gas station filling up my car. Another customer approached me and asked if I needed assistance. I didn't think I was having trouble but they obviously did. Here I was thinking I was hiding my disease and doing well, but this complete stranger was asking if I needed help. I could have been annoyed by this interaction but instead I was completely fine with it. If anything, I welcomed the opportunity to speak to someone I didn't know, and turned the moment into a teachable lesson about my condition and about Parkinson's.

I've come to realize that living with Parkinson's (or other physically debilitating diseases) means every day you are on display. Parkinson's is a transparent illness, there's no hiding from it. My symptoms have progressed to the point that I can no longer conceal them. More frequent and more severe tremors, stiffness and rigidity of body movement, paralysis of facial muscles, impaired speech, an incapability to form words quickly, slurring of speech, dragging of feet, less frequent blinking–these are all symptoms of my advancing PD. These symptoms are clearly on display for everyone to see. I'm no longer naive or in denial about this. I've accepted that people can tell something is different about me just by looking at me. I see the puzzled looks on people's faces as they try to decipher what my physical ailment may be. I've made the choice to not be bothered by this which makes me feel empowered, not ashamed, by my adversity.

While I don't let people's inquisitiveness about my health bother me, I'm fully aware this may not be easy for everyone–especially for those in the early stages of their diagnosis. I've heard people say they resent strangers for openly gawking at them as though they were a caged animal in a zoo. I get it. Not everyone is comfortable being an ambassador for what ails them. But take my word for it—once you let go of any anger or resentment stemming from people's curiosity about your situation, life will feel easier.

Just the other day I went zip-lining and noticed the company employees watching me and then exchanging confused looks. It didn't offend me in the least. I approached them and said, *"If you're wondering why my leg is shaking it's because I have Parkinson's disease."* This immediately put them at ease and started a dialogue. Our brief conversation forever shattered their ingrained stereotype of what someone with Parkinson's disease can and cannot do. That wouldn't have happened had I not been open to discussing my illness.

I recognize doing this may be especially difficult if you're a private person. It may feel uncomfortable exposing your medical diagnosis to strangers, but as with most things in life, practice and repeated attempts will help. Trust me, in time, the awkwardness melts away. Acknowledging your life has either temporarily changed, or is forever altered, is the first step to feeling more comfortable with your situation. Only once you've accepted this can you move forward in a healthy and positive way, which includes being comfortable sharing your journey with others.

Talking about your challenges, vocalizing your ailments, and discussing what is troubling you, can ease your emotional burden. Trust me when I tell you that once you start speaking about your ordeal and start sharing your feelings with others, it will lessen your suffering. Your problems won't magically go away, but they won't seem as unbearable or as hopeless as they may have if you were struggling alone. Share your experience with others. Tell as many people as will listen. There is power in saying the words aloud and having others hear them. The old cliché is true—sharing your hardship with others often halves the weight of the burden. It's a lesson that took me many years to understand and hone.

CHAPTER EIGHT
Get smart—knowledge is power

I'm not proud to admit this—when I was first diagnosed with Parkinson's in 2015, I didn't want to know anything about the disease, and I absolutely did not want to know what the future would hold. I thought ignorance was bliss. I was 56 years old and feared that if I learned about possible impending symptoms, it would be so devastating it would impact my then present-life. I basically stuck my head in the sand hoping change wasn't coming. You'd think I'd want to learn everything I could about the disease, to better prepare for what was to come, but that wasn't the case. I didn't even want to meet other people who had PD because I wrongly assumed my experience would be unique, and I felt I would not, and could not, relate to others who were also suffering from Parkinson's.

It's embarrassing to admit this, but when I was first diagnosed with PD, I naively thought I could beat the disease. I had so few symptoms. My attitude was: *Bring it Parkinson's, give me your best shot 'cause whatever you do I'm going to defeat you.* I genuinely thought I would be the first person in history to defeat Parkinson's. I was going to show the world how easy that feat would be. I know it sounds cocky. I think it was a subconscious defense mechanism my brain used to trick me into believing everything would be OK, because at the time, the alternative felt impossible for me to accept or comprehend. As my symptoms progressed, that attitude didn't last too long, and I quickly realized Parkinson's was going to be the battle of my life. Any major crisis has a way of taking you down a notch, and Parkinson's certainly humbled me.

These days, I seek credible sources like local, regional and national Parkinson's organizations and attempt to learn as much as I possibly can about the disease; I'm a sponge trying to soak it all up. I now believe knowledge is power, and getting smart about whatever we're experiencing is a way of gaining or taking control of our situation.

Knowing what may be around the corner of my Parkinson's journey motivates me to stay in the present and do things today that I otherwise may have put off. This disease doesn't allow for procrastination because you never know when you'll no longer be able to do the things you once loved, or the things you've dreamed of doing. PD takes a piece of you every day, which means tomorrow may be worse than today. Don't put anything off or save it for another day because you don't know when your abilities will suddenly be tarnished. Carpe diem: seize the day.

I took up Spartan obstacle course racing because I knew as my symptoms progressed, my participation would eventually become limited.

Knowing what to expect in terms of how your illness will affect your body and overall health, removes the element of surprise once it actually occurs. Knowing or predicting something before it happens takes away its power. If you know it's "normal" then it will likely be less upsetting to face, and you may be better prepared to deal with it. This is why I say knowledge is power. There is no sense in being caught off guard.

If you're caught off guard when the change happens, or if you know it's coming but still feel saddened by it, that's OK too. Don't be hard on yourself. We all process things at a different pace, but hopefully the awareness may soften the blow, even just a little bit.

I was warned Parkinson's would one day take away my ability to get dressed by myself, I just never imagined it would happen as early as it did. Within six years of my diagnosis, at age 63, I began struggling with basic tasks like buttoning my shirt or zipping up my pants. Once it started happening it progressed rapidly.

Another unwelcome challenge Parkinson's brings is constipation. Man, how I hoped this was one PD symptom that would skip me, but sadly that wasn't the case. So, when I started having bathroom issues, as uncomfortable as it was, I didn't panic and worry it was caused by another ailment. As unpleasant as it was to think about, I was glad to be in the know.

As helpful as it is to be aware of the symptoms, you may still be caught off guard when they begin or be stunned by their severity. Even though I knew I'd eventually have mobility issues, it was shocking when certain disabilities kicked in. At age 63, I could roll over in bed. Within one year I couldn't do that anymore and it was quite surprising the first time it happened. I was shocked by this loss, because it was so easy before Parkinson's, I never gave it a second thought. But now that ability is taken away, it's a huge challenge. I'm also having balance issues and dragging my feet when I walk. I know that in the future my walking abilities will worsen even further. It's kinda hard to imagine what that will look like for me, and I don't know how soon it will happen, but at least it won't be a complete shock.

For me, knowing what will eventually happen makes me want to do as much as I can today, because I know I may not be able to do it tomorrow. Fear of missing out (FOMO, as the young kids like to call it) gives you the kick in the butt to get things done and not put anything off.

When people recently diagnosed with Parkinson's ask me for advice about how to deal with life going forward, I always emphasize the following:

1. Research your illness.
2. Consult a medical physician, and specifically a neurologist, as they will guide and help you through this process.
3. Take the meds you need but also inquire about antidepressants. If you don't need them right now, that's great, but chances are you'll need them in the future. Better to have a prescription on hand for when the dark clouds start to appear.
4. Speak to a therapist or a psychologist. You'll need professional guidance to navigate the emotional part of this journey.

5. A speech therapist is also useful, as you'll likely lose the ability to move your mouth, tongue, and lips, and in time it'll become increasingly difficult to speak.

6. Physical exercise is a must. In my case, working out helps stress my central nervous system, which in turn helps set back my Parkinson's symptoms. After a few hours at the gym, I'm less rigid and my gait is improved. This only lasts a few hours, but during that time I feel as though I have paused my Parkinson's clock. It's unlikely everyone will have the same experience, but either way, physical exercise is crucial for a healthy body and mind. It doesn't matter what kind of exercise you choose, whether it's walking, running, yoga, or in my case, weightlifting, just do something physically active. If you aren't exercising you're automatically losing the battle with Parkinson's disease.

7. A healthy diet is essential. Now more than ever, what you put in your body is important.

8. Seek help and find allies—this may range from confiding in a loved one to joining a support group.

Many of the above suggestions can help anyone diagnosed with a debilitating medical illness.

It's taken seven years into my Parkinson's before I needed a speech therapist. My voice was weakening more and more and my words began to slur. I knew I needed to do something about it. I regret not seeing a speech therapist earlier. I recommend looking into one at the first signs of speech difficulty (slurred words, weak voice, etc.). It came on so suddenly for me–one day I noticed I was slurring. It was another thing interrupting my life. I forgot to take care of my mouth while I was using exercise to help the rest of my body deal with PD.

I can't say enough how important physical exercise is. I was blown away the day I realized weight training seemed to reverse my mobility problems. It was like a new lease on life! Even my trainer was shocked. We had no idea that the heavy weight training would help me to stand upright, and walk faster without the foot shuffle. For the first time since my diagnosis I felt new hope in managing Parkinson's.

Because of my athletic lifestyle, I've always had a healthy diet, concentrating on whole foods and 90% clean eating, with no sugar. Since healthy eating was always part of my life, I didn't have to make changes once I was diagnosed. There are some diet strategies around Parkinson's, such as drinking more fluids and eating more fibre to help ease constipation, for example. Talk with your medical team about specifics for you.

For those like me dealing with Parkinson's disease, I also recommend consulting a physician to discuss whether deep brain stimulation (DBS) may help.

DBS is the most-performed surgical treatment for Parkinson's. It works by having thin metal wires (called leads or electrodes) placed in the brain. The leads receive mild electrical stimulation from a small pulse-generator (a pacemaker-like device) implanted in the chest. The electrical pulses are sent to the brain to help control some motor symptoms. In a nutshell, DBS directly changes brain activity in a controlled manner. DBS doesn't cure PD symptoms, but it can decrease the need for medications and improve quality of life.

DBS surgery wasn't an avenue for my personal PD journey (at present my tremors are not as severe as they are for others). However, I've seen the results of DBS surgery firsthand and know that for some PD sufferers who are experiencing severe tremors, DBS may be a game changer. Having said that, although the surgery has been transformative for many people with PD, it isn't for everyone. Since I'm not a doctor I encourage you to consult your physician to discuss whether it may be an option for you.

As I mentioned in an earlier chapter, I strongly encourage people recently diagnosed with PD to join a Parkinson's support group as soon as possible. There are people in these groups who have lived with the disease much longer than you have and their experience will likely help you navigate this illness. Also, the emotional support they may offer is invaluable and can help keep you from feeling you're battling this disease alone.

Initially after my diagnosis, I wasn't ready to join those groups. But now at year seven of living with Parkinson's it's very beneficial for me to be involved with the support groups. Many cities have a PD support group and there are countless resources online, so there's no excuse for not reaching out to one of these organizations. Trust me—it will help.

My situation was unique—I didn't join a Parkinson's support group but instead eventually created my own group. It wasn't something I consciously sought out, but something that happened organically through social media and through the connections I've made. In 2021, the documentary film, *It's Just Parkinson's,* was made about my Parkinson's journey and the IJP mindset was introduced to a larger group of people. The core themes of IJP resonated with audiences and they embraced the IJP way of thinking. Before I knew it, I was leading a community of like-minded people from around the globe. Again, this wasn't something I sought out, but if it will help inspire others with their own Parkinson's journey, I'm happy to share my experience and my outlook on battling this disease.

CHAPTER NINE
How Parkinson's has enriched my life

What I'm about to say may be shocking and leave you wondering if I've lost my mind, but trust me, I haven't. I genuinely believe the following confession to be true: being diagnosed with Parkinson's disease has been the worst thing that's ever happened to me—*and* it has also made my life better.

If you think that statement is unbelievable, brace yourselves because there's more! I also believe having PD has made me a better person. While I'm fully aware it's a life-changing and debilitating disease, I don't see having Parkinson's as being all bad, because it's not. I say this, and truly believe it, because at the end of the day having PD has made me a better version of myself.

Before I was diagnosed with Parkinson's disease I was not as empathetic, caring, open, and vulnerable as I currently am. Parkinson's helped me connect with these parts of my personality and brought them to the surface. I use the word *helps* purposely because it is a benefit. I'm not saying I wasn't a kind or compassionate individual before my diagnosis, just that these qualities have been amplified since my disease materialized.

I think the main catalyst for this character change is the wonderful people I've met on my journey. Had I not been diagnosed with PD it's very unlikely I would've crossed paths with dozens of fellow Parkinson's sufferers from around the world, who I've bonded with—either in real life or through social media—and consider my new friends. I cannot, nor do I want to, imagine my life without these people. Their friendship and support are gifts I cherish and for which I will be forever grateful.

Another way this adversity has improved my life is by putting my existence into perspective. Being diagnosed with an incurable illness often forces people to face their mortality, but that doesn't have to be a negative or depressing thing. Facing your mortality in a positive way may help you better appreciate your life. Realizing I'll eventually lose my battle with PD makes me want to live life to the fullest. Knowing that over time my mobility will greatly deteriorate, makes me want to do as many things as I can *now*, in the present, so I no longer put anything off.

Ever since I can remember I've revered vintage American muscle cars. My uncle had a 1967 Chevrolet Camaro I was envious of growing up. As a kid I always dreamed of buying that same vehicle when I was old enough to drive. What the younger version of me could never imagine was that I would own two muscle cars in my life.

The first was a 1968 Dodge Charger–that car was great! It was in good condition, it ran beautifully, and it was fast—maybe too fast. I bought the car when I was 17 years old, a junior in high school. I had acquired my driver's license the year before, yet somehow I got my parents to believe I needed this car. As I said, the car was fast. Hell, it looked like it was doing 100 mph when it was standing still.

Sadly, the dream was short-lived. The day after I bought it I took it out to show off to all my friends and promptly got a ticket for racing on a public highway. I lost my license for nine months–practically my entire senior year of high school. And let me tell you, in high school no license = no dates. To make matters even worse, my parents made me sell the car!

Almost 50 years later I purchased my second muscle car, a 1969 Camaro. The car was completely rebuilt from the ground up. I was so excited to go see it—I had to fly to Atlanta to check it out. When I sat in it and turned the key, I had no more negotiating leverage at all! The look on my face must have been priceless. This car was *mine*. I absolutely love driving it. The car is fast, but now I feel no urgency to prove it. Besides, my driving abilities aren't what they used to be—LOL.

The lesson in my 1969 Camaro story is you should do what you love before Parkinson's takes your ability away. I know at some point in the future I'll lose the ability to drive. That didn't stop me from going out and buying that dream muscle car. I might as well enjoy it while I can. I encourage everyone to follow that same philosophy—enjoy it (whatever your "it" is) while you can.

Another lesson this disease has taught me is that helping others gives you purpose, and we all need purpose in life–it's what gets us out of bed in the morning. It's important to avoid using your illness or hardship as an excuse; strive to find ways to help and to be of service to others. People often make the mistake of thinking that giving back solely involves a monetary exchange. Donating money is absolutely a wonderful way to give back to your community, but it's by no means the only way.

Being a role model, a good parent/spouse/friend/neighbor, etc.—all these actions can give you purpose in life. Building and sustaining healthy relationships can help build your self-esteem, which is a prime example of how helping others often ends up benefiting ourselves.

People going through difficulties often put on blinders and all they focus on are their own problems. It's understandable to feel all-consumed when you're facing a hardship or illness, but this shouldn't be an excuse for not being of service to others. Although you're going through a time of need, so are many others in your community, and possibly even in your inner circle. Try not to micro-focus on your own life to the point you forget or neglect those around you.

I've seen firsthand how the person doing the *helping* is often themselves being *helped* in the process. As my illness progressed, I took the time to get closer to my caregiver, Pattie. It's not as if we'd grown apart before my diagnosis; our relationship was just different pre-diagnosis. We came into the relationship as equals, each of us bringing our specialness to this wonderful union. Two adults equally contributing emotionally, spiritually, and physically to the relationship. That's shifted since my diagnosis. Pattie shoulders much of the load now. Yet rather than it driving us apart, it has created the opportunity to talk openly and honestly about all subjects. Nothing is off-limits. We've become closer as a result and our relationship is impervious to any destructive force. Thank you, Parkinson's!

Non-Parkinson's friendships have become more meaningful to me than ever. They were always important, but now they've become an emotional and physical pillar in my life. Parkinson's gives me a sense of urgency. My abilities are waning, and I want to ensure my friends understand their critical role in this wonderful life journey. These friends may be called upon to do things typical friends wouldn't be asked to do. I now have trouble undoing my pants. When I go to the bathroom things can get urgent as I fumble to unbutton my jeans. More than once I've had to ask for help when I needed to go badly. It certainly provides an intimacy in a male friendship not normally found in the men's room, and when it happened to me, we certainly laughed about it. I think if you're matter-of-fact about it, it's no big deal.

The founding and emergence of IJP has made a profound impact on many people–me included. IJP's creation stems directly from me being stricken by Parkinson's. Although IJP is life-altering, it wouldn't exist if I didn't have Parkinson's. Amazing, isn't it? IJP is the main reason I can say Parkinson's has made my life better.

My good friend Brian doesn't have Parkinson's and yet IJP has had an impact on his life. He uses the mindset to help him navigate difficult situations in his life. IJP is bigger than Parkinson's. Brian understands it. He's joined the IJP family and you can too.

CHAPTER TEN
Never give up—never surrender

In the past few years many people have told me they've been inspired by the way I've conducted myself in my battle against Parkinson's disease. I am deeply humbled by such feedback. These same people have encouraged me to keep talking about my journey and to continue sharing my experiences with others. Their kindness and compassion have encouraged and allowed me to be candid and vulnerable while writing this book.

Although this book has discussed my personal experiences with this incurable disease, it's been inspired by all the fellow PD sufferers I've met over the years, as well as anyone grappling with adversity. I hope you've found reading this book useful, and even recognized versions of your story in its pages.

Whether it's through this book, the documentary film, *It's Just Parkinson's,* or any of my social media platforms (www.itsjustparkinsons.com and @itsjustparkinsons on Instagram), the message I aim to share and instill in others is always the same: **never give up, never surrender.** As long as you're breathing you are still in the fight.

One of my favorite words in the English language is *grit*. Besides my mantra, "It's Just Parkinson's" (IJP), the word grit is one that often comes to mind. Grit can be defined as passion and perseverance for long-term and meaningful goals, even when faced with obstacles. I strive to live my life with grit to ensure my journey has direction and meaning. I believe these aspirations give my existence continued purpose.

What also gives me great purpose are the people I've met during my Parkinson's journey. I have been humbled beyond words by the messages of support and admiration I've received from individuals around the world.

A young man named Patrick, aged twenty-six, from Fort Myers, Florida reached out to me. He told me that since his father was diagnosed with PD, his dad was feeling defeated and had completely given up on life. After he showed his father my documentary film, his dad was motivated to get up off the couch and go for a walk for the first time in years. I'm beyond humbled that my story inspired such change, but what I say to this man's father is that I in turn am inspired by him! He made a conscious choice to get back into the fight. I think that's remarkable.

I also heard about a local man named Matt, age forty-nine, who was depressed about having Parkinson's for the past seven years. A friend knew him and told him he needed to talk to me. I met him at a local restaurant where we bonded immediately. We talked about Parkinson's for over an hour, we cried together, and I knew I had a friend for life. He has completely changed his outlook on life—he now goes camping with his family, and has a new IJP tattoo!

If you've taken a break from battling your adversity, or if you've completely stopped fighting because you think there is no hope, then listen up: there is always hope! I've heard it said that hope dies last. Giving up is exactly what Parkinson's wants you to do. You can't lose if you don't quit! Reset your journey and start with a single first step.

Over the years, my Parkinson's journey has been sidetracked a few times. I reset my journey by reimmersing myself in the IJP mindset. This may work for you, or you may need to reach out to family, close friends or PD organizations. The point is: we all fall down. The important part is to stand back UP.

I want to let you in on a secret: if you're fighting Parkinson's or any other type of illness or adversity, you are *my* everyday hero. Your will to battle and not give up in the face of adversity is nothing short of remarkable. You are stronger than you think and I am inspired by YOU. Whether they are daily chores or colossal accomplishments, every day I'm inspired by stories of what people with PD are achieving. We are breaking the mold and quashing stereotypes of what people with Parkinson's disease can and cannot do. We all deserve to be commended for this. We are changing lives simply by challenging the limitations set by past generations, and in turn we're paving a new way forward for future generations of PD sufferers.

By continuing to fight through your adversity, you will be the best version of yourself. Keep focusing on your own journey and on being true to yourself. The only person to compare yourself against is the one in the mirror. Maybe you can't lift 450-pound weights as I can, but you don't have to be as strong as me to have strength. Having strength isn't about lifting heavy things; it's about having courage and continuing to fight with grit.

I encourage you to do the best you can with what you've got, at whatever stage of life you are in. Be the best warrior you can be. If you give up, then it *is* hopeless. Stay in the fight. There is always hope as long as you keep fighting.

I never set out to write a book about living with Parkinson's disease. Never in my wildest imagination did I think this would be part of my journey. Over the years I've met some truly amazing people who are also fighting this disease. They encouraged me tell my story and share my tips for how to live a healthy, meaningful life despite the adversity of Parkinson's disease. Being told I have an important story worth sharing was humbling. After a lot of soul-searching, I decided to take on this endeavor. So here I am, stepping up to the metaphorical podium and accepting the role of PD ambassador and role model.

When I was younger, and long before my Parkinson's diagnosis, I enjoyed reading books about people put into situations where the outcome was in doubt. *I Play to Win* by Freddie Steinmark, *Find a Way* by Diana Nyad, *Between a Rock and a Hard Place* by Aron Ralston, and the biography of Ernest Shackleton by Roland Huntford are among my faves. Little did I know then that this boyhood fascination would be a very important tool I'd carry with me, and that would guide me once I was diagnosed with PD. It laid the foundation for the mindset I choose to live by, and I tend to approach everything I do with the same ethos.

It's remarkable what the human body and spirit are capable of when faced with true adversity. Aron Ralston is the perfect example of this. I'm not exactly sure when I first became familiar with his story, but I was immediately inspired by his plight. He's a warrior in the truest sense of the word, and the epitome of grit and never-surrender attitude. The feat he accomplished to save his life is beyond extraordinary!

In 2003, while canyoneering solo in the remote Bluejohn Canyon in eastern Utah, Aron dislodged a boulder which promptly pinned his right arm under the rock. He remained calm and didn't panic. He got as comfortable as he could and studied his options, which were limited. He knew he had told no one where he was going, and being found by other hikers was unlikely. With no way of sending out a distress single he knew the chances of being found by a rescue team were slim to none. It quickly became clear to Aron he was the only one who could get himself out of this situation.

After being trapped for six days, Aron realized the only way to escape and survive was to amputate part of his right arm. Remarkably, that's exactly what he did—using a dull multi-tool blade! He then rappelled down a six-story cliff and began the 8-mile hike back to his truck. After six miles he fortunately ran into some hikers who called for help. A rescue helicopter ultimately picked him up and flew him to a hospital. You can read his autobiographical book *Between a Rock and a Hard Place*, or watch *127 Hours*, the surprisingly true-to-life film about his misadventure.

Aron Ralston's calm demeanor in the face of certain death was nothing less than heroic. His story should be an inspiration to everyone, regardless of what kind of hardship you're facing. His attitude was not, "*Why me?*" but rather, "*What now?*" I try putting myself in his shoes and think about what I would do if I were in that same predicament. The main lesson for me with such inspiring stories is that the ability to persevere, and a calm, cool, mindset, are the keys to escaping certain defeat. It's a lesson we can all use when faced with our own adversity. That's true grit—to know that death is imminent and likely unavoidable, and yet continue fighting to end up rewriting your own history.

Another person I admire greatly is Diana Nyad. At the age of 64, when most people are thinking about retirement or slowing down, Diana became the first person to swim from Cuba to Key West, Florida, without the aid of a shark cage. Diana had failed during four previous attempts, but in 2013, after almost 53 hours of grueling swimming, she ultimately accomplished her goal. Her tenacity, grit, and perseverance are nothing short of astonishing.

Diana's memoir is entitled *Find a Way*, and before I came up with the term, "It's Just Parkinson's," I adopted her mantra for inspiration as I attempted some of my own epic feats, such as bicycling the French Pyrenees and competing in Spartan races. I vividly recall many Spartan races where I would whisper to myself, "*Find a way,*" to motivate myself to keep going. During those moments it felt as though Diana was right beside me cheering me on.

I met Diana in 2018. The encounter was exciting but equally nerve-racking. How many people get to meet one of their real-life heroes? When I met her, the emotions that had built up, during all those races she helped me through, came crashing down and I simply lost it. I couldn't speak; heck, I could barely whisper. I basically cried during the entire interaction, and she was extremely gracious and caring toward me.

I have such admiration for Diana Nyad and what she's accomplished as being the first and only person to swim non-stop from Cuba to Florida, which took 52hrs, 54mins. And one that took 5 attempts, which she began at age 28. She never gave up. An impressive feat at any age. I think of her often, and use her story as an example, and a reminder of how powerful the human body, mind, and spirit are.

We may not ultimately conquer everything we set our sights on—heck, I wish I could just button up my shirt every morning—but at the very least we must try. Try and try and try again. If we don't succeed, that's OK. What's not OK is not giving it our best shot.

There are many lessons I've learned since my Parkinson's diagnosis. Here are just a few:

1. Overall, a positive attitude in the face of this disease is critical.
2. Own your disease. Don't hide it. Tell people about it.
3. Wear your Parkinson's like a badge of honor. You've not been inflicted, you've been chosen!
4. Fight this disease at every turn.
5. Find an exercise that helps you in your Parkinson's battle.
6. Once you start exercising, don't stop moving!
7. Parkinson's is a team sport—seek support from a wide range of allies and get involved with support groups.

8. If you're fortunate enough to have a caregiver, make sure to honor them. Remember, you're in this together.
9. Live the best life you can. Parkinson's is not a death sentence.
10. Embrace the tenants of IJP: ROCK + LIGHT + HOPE = INSPIRED, FOCUSED, UNSTOPPABLE.

It's been seven years since my Parkinson's diagnosis. I've learned a lot since then and expect to learn much more down the road. It hasn't always been a smooth journey, but I'm proud to say I'm still in the fight. I know in the end Parkinson's is a losing battle, yet I feel I am overcoming it at every turn.

Parkinson's is a debilitating illness, there is no getting around it. But like most things in life, it's not one-dimensional; like an onion, it has many layers. For me, Parkinson's has been my teacher, my friend and foe, my constant companion, my worst nightmare, and the sweetest surprise. I don't see Parkinson's as a chain around my neck but rather as my superpower, because as I've mentioned in a previous chapter, I believe my illness has made me a better person.

I joke with my family and friends that if I was a superhero I would be called *The Shuffler,* because I can no longer lift my feet when I walk, so my feet make a loud shuffling sound. That's another lesson this disease has taught me, the importance of not taking oneself too seriously—there is great healing in laughter and humor.

Parkinson's has also taught me that no matter the hardship, with the IJP mindset (inspired, focused, unstoppable), I'm unbreakable. It may get dark and at times seem impossible to move forward, but with a warrior attitude I'll rise to meet any challenge Parkinson's throws my way.

As the son of a U.S. Marine, I gravitate toward military or war analogies. I'm particularly inspired by the idea of a soldier lying in a foxhole who is surrounded by the enemy. That soldier has a choice—to simply go down, or go down fighting. Either way their destiny is the same, so why not choose the latter? That's how I see my illness, I choose to go down fighting.

If you ever find yourself in one of life's foxholes, I hope you choose to go down fighting.

CHAPTER ELEVEN
A caregiver's perspective
by Pattie Stoffel

Of all the possibilities I thought of when I first met John, being a caregiver to a Parkinson's patient was not even on my radar. As it is with most couples, we were focused on the good things our relationship was going to bring. The heart of our conversations centered on the exciting journey we were embarking on as a couple. We saw nothing but blue sky and open roads as we looked ahead.

For eight years our life was fairly carefree. That all changed the day John came home from a grueling cycling vacation in the French Pyrenees mountains. He confided to me he thought something was wrong with his body. During the trip he'd felt a weakness in his right side. I was concerned but not overly worried. After all, he'd just finished an extremely demanding bicycle ride and was in peak physical condition.

John's course of action consisted of mainly ignoring his symptoms. It took him well over a year before he could no

longer ignore his symptoms and had to confront them—
something was wrong with his body. He reluctantly made
an appointment with a neurologist to get an answer. The
diagnosis: Parkinson's.

John's initial reaction was one of bravado. After all, he'd
faced and crushed many physical challenges in his lifetime.
I think he figured Parkinson's was just like every other
challenge. He'd do some extra sit-ups, maybe a handful of
push-ups, and go out and take Parkinson's down. He even
told me he was going to be the first person ever to defeat
Parkinson's. John was practically writing his Nobel Prize
acceptance speech.

Obviously, none of that happened. Over the course of six
months his bravado gave way to denial. Which ultimately
led to acceptance.

As time went on, his symptoms became more prevalent. In
the span of five years his symptoms went from moderately
noticeable, to in some cases, debilitating. My role as a
caregiver mirrored his worsening symptoms. As he lost
abilities, I took on more responsibilities. In our relationship,
we generally split the load of household tasks 50/50, with
John picking up things like finances, home repairs, car
maintenance, lawn care, pool maintenance, grilling, etc.
Today that split of responsibilities is about 80/20. John helps
where he can, but in many cases he is unable to complete
the task without my assistance.

I know my caregiver role will broaden as John's abilities
continue to decline. I'm fully committed to my expanding
role. As such, I'm preparing NOW for that eventuality. I'm
making sure I am ready physically and mentally to accept

what's coming. There are several things I do to keep myself primed: I work out, I get out with friends, I engage in self-care (tub soaks, pedicures, etc.), in addition to having "me" time. I'm also learning as much as I can about what's to come with Parkinson's via reading, podcasts, support groups, etc. Finally, John and I continually discuss the need for outside third-party care, and when that may become necessary.

John's illness clarifies my role as a caregiver. Many will say he's in the fight of his life. I beg to differ. From my perspective, WE are in the fight of our life!! As John often says, "Parkinson's is a team sport." That's where I come in. I support our "team" as we navigate the stages of his Parkinson's. I've been here since day one and have suffered, alongside John, every setback Parkinson's has thrown at him. Like John, I will never give up the fight, nor surrender to Parkinson's. John has vowed to go down swinging. That heroic statement guides my efforts. I will do what it takes, right beside him, to assist in his battle.

The other day I overheard a conversation in which one person exclaimed, "For better or for worse." I concluded she was repeating her wedding vows and lamenting her circumstances. I thought about it for a moment and concluded that wasn't how I looked at our Parkinson's situation. To me it's not better or worse, it's just different. A path we never intended to take. It's the odyssey we're on now.

I try not to dwell on things I can't control. For the most part, I'm successful. But there are times when the totality of the situation knocks me down. At those times I think of John and all he goes through fighting Parkinson's every single day. That thought bolsters my spirit and carries me forward. He's my hero. My knight in shining armor. The man of my dreams. If he can do it I can do it.

Don't get me wrong, this situation sucks. Do I sometimes wish I didn't have to go on this journey? Hell yes! Are there times when the whole situation overwhelms me, and I want to run and hide? You're damn right. Would I rather be lying on a beach somewhere drinking a margarita? Don't get me started.

One powerful technique I use every day is visualization. In my mind's eye I see my future self being even stronger (mentally and physically) than I am today. This relieves some of the anxiety associated with the unknown future. I don't dread the future and in a strange way I look forward to meeting the stronger me.

Another technique I employ is optimism. I've been optimistic my entire life. No matter what challenges occurred I was confident I could handle the particular issue and the outcome would be positive. I find it critical to use optimism in dealing with Parkinson's.

And optimism is contagious. I find it helps me cope with the situation and that helps John cope too. Don't get me wrong, I'm realistic about the ultimate outcome of Parkinson's, but I don't need to drag that weight around every single day. Being optimistic brightens my day and creates a positive pathway for us to move forward.

Patience is an attitude I feel is critical in dealing with Parkinson's. Due to our situation, it's easy to become overwhelmed and angry. As bumps in the road occur, I try not to lose my temper and criticize John's mishaps. John now routinely has accidents throughout the day: spilling his protein drinks on the floor, dropping food on the furniture, clogging the toilet, or misplacing valuables like his wallet and glasses. In the grand scheme of things these are minor issues. Keeping them in perspective as they occur helps maintain a positive atmosphere in our lives.

Finally, I believe effective time management is super critical. Failure to manage my time properly leads to disaster and ruins our day. Every day I wake up before John and make a list of the tasks and appointments we need to address that day. This gives me a head start on the day, and allows me to be available to John when he wakes up. Effective time management provides me the ability to anticipate and address John's needs, especially first thing in the morning (getting dressed, tying shoes, making breakfast, etc.).

I've been asked many times what my typical day looks like. There is no typical day when dealing with Parkinson's. Much of what occurs during the day is dictated by how John feels and his levels of rigidity, balance, walking, and speech. Any issue John has that I didn't anticipate will definitely throw a wrench in that day's activities. Given those facts, here is a general look at what a typical day for me looks like:

1. I wake up before John and identify tasks for the day.
2. I identify how John feels when he wakes up. This dictates whether the tasks I anticipated will be addressed.
3. I help John get out of bed and dressed for the day.
4. I organize John's medication regimen for the day.
5. While John has breakfast and addresses that day's task, I go to the gym. While I'm out I also run any errands required.

6. The rest of the day is spent with John and addressing that day's tasks and any related Parkinson's issues.

I want everyone to know one of the most effective ways we handle Parkinson's is through laughter.

John and I continually find humor in dealing with Parkinson's. We find ourselves laughing every morning as I help him dress. We shrug our shoulders and smirk throughout the day when accidents occur. Laughter truly is the best medicine and I recommend healthy doses of it every single day. For us, laughter makes the impossible possible.

I'M STILL HERE

A poem by John Cullen

Pieces missing.

Lost to eternity.

Stumbling.

Shuffling.

Stooping.

More to go.

You're always taking.

*Yet I rise knowing you will never have what you
ultimately came to take.*

Me.

I'm still here.

I'm still me.

APPENDIX

Sometimes I find myself wondering what kind of advice I would give my younger self, if I could. If time machines were invented, and I could go back a decade or two, what would I tell the younger version of me, the one whose life has yet to be affected by PD, and who doesn't have a care in the world about what the future may bring?

It's been quite the year. I know people often say this, but for me it's particularly true. This last year, in 2023, my Parkinson's really changed me, more than any previous year. It's not just the physical changes, even though there have been many. It's changed my outlook and my day-to-day life.

In the past year, three words have literally changed my life: It's Just Parkinson's (IJP). Although they started taking root many years ago, it's during the past year they've really taken shape. They've evolved into more than just a life motto; it's become a movement.

In the past year, IJP has gone from a state of mind to a revolution. It has inspired healthy people and Parkinson's sufferers alike. And although I never wanted or expected to be a role model, I humbly accept the task if it means helping others by sharing my story. I mean that literally, since my life story inspired the production of a documentary film, which in the first year of release has been viewed by hundreds of people.

So, you see, it truly has been quite the year.

But I can't help thinking back even further, to where this journey really started. The term "journey" is quite fitting, as this all started in 2014 on another continent, in a foreign land, while bike riding down grueling mountain terrain in the French Pyrenees. I was oblivious to it all then, to how my life was about to change forever, for worse, yet in a way, for better.

If I knew then what I know now, I'd probably write a letter to myself that went something like this:

A letter to my younger self

Dear John,

It's 2014 and you're 55 years old. You have a great life, but it's about to change in ways you never imagined. It's OK if you're scared. It's OK if you're angry. All feelings are valid.

But I won't sugarcoat it: this fight will be long, and it will be hard. Your body will betray you. After years of training and working out, your body will give up on you and basic tasks will seem impossible.

There will be days when you don't recognize yourself and you'll doubt your identity. There will also come a time when you have more bad days than good days, and you'll wonder what's the point of living.

Don't be scared. Don't give up. And absolutely never say die. You got this. TRUST ME.

Once you're diagnosed with Parkinson's disease (PD for short), you'll forever think of your life in two parts: life before Parkinson's and life with Parkinson's. Before and after.

BEFORE: will be your past life, a time when "Parkinson's" wasn't part of your lexicon.

Life before Parkinson's was a time when you attempted anything without a thought or care of physical limitations. It was a time when you never contemplated failure. You rode your bicycle an insane number of miles, in all kinds of conditions, and on all kinds of terrain. You ran outrageous distances with limited training. You simply willed your body to do what you wanted it to do, and it responded. In addition to running and cycling, you climbed mountains, parasailed, and participated in CrossFit. You never worried about how your body would react because you didn't need to. It did what you told it to do. Period.

AFTER: is the future I'm writing to you from. It's life with Parkinson's and (SPOILER ALERT!) it will be OK.

You'll be diagnosed with Parkinson's in 2015 at age 56, but even before then you'll suspect something is wrong. Odd symptoms will plague you for months, You'll find yourself researching diseases like multiple sclerosis (MS) and Parkinson's disease (PD), all while secretly hoping you are terribly wrong. But even after the official diagnosis, your symptoms will be minimal (at first). You'll look and feel healthy, and no one will believe you have PD. Their disbelief will rub off on you and you'll wonder if maybe the doctors got it wrong, and it's a mistaken diagnosis.

When these moments come, don't dwell on them, because they are false hope. In time more Parkinson's symptoms will crop up and you'll no longer have the luxury of doubt. There'll come a day when not even an hour will pass without being reminded of your PD. It will be your constant companion.

Don't hide your diagnosis. Tell everyone you have Parkinson's. Don't be ashamed of it, own it! Doing this will take the stigma out of it. If you appear comfortable discussing it, people will in turn be comfortable asking you questions, and they will educate themselves in the process. Encourage a dialogue. Whether you want to or not, you are now a "Parkinson's Ambassador." Take up the mantle with pride.

In time, many of your abilities will diminish, some sooner than you expect or are ready for. On countless mornings you'll have trouble just getting out of bed. Your walk will suddenly become a shuffle and you'll jokingly compare yourself to Frankenstein. Your dexterity will take a hit: simple tasks like buttoning and unbuttoning shirts will seem impossible, and steak knives will suddenly become unusable. Some days, getting dressed without help will seem hopeless. It's OK. Ask and accept help when you need it—there is no shame in it.

You may need assistance with certain things but that doesn't mean you're incapable. Everyone has limitations.

Be gentle with yourself. Don't allow yourself to get upset about your fate. Never blame yourself or get angry if you can't do something. Learn to roll with whatever Parkinson's dishes out. I know that's easier said than done, but a positive attitude truly is half the battle, and you, my dear John, have always been optimistic. No matter the situation, you've always looked on the bright side, so never lose hold of that hopefulness.

You've always loved physical activity. The gym has been a form of therapy, but make friends with all forms of therapy. Invest in occupational therapy and even speech therapy, as they will be of great benefit on this journey.

Due to Parkinson's physical symptoms (shakiness, stiffness, difficulty walking, problems with balance and coordination) many people wrongly assume PD only affects the body's movement. Don't fall into this trap. Parkinson's is a neurological brain disorder and how it will affect your mind may be the biggest surprise of all. Depression and suicidal thoughts are real. Focus on your mental health as much as your physical health, for you can't be healthy without both.

There will come a day when you say, *"I'm John Cullen. I f-ing got this. Bring it on Parkinson's! Give me your best shot!"* When that time comes, hang on to that warrior attitude because you'll need it in the future where I am (and beyond). A word of caution: be careful what you wish for because Parkinson's will certainly "bring it."

In time, you'll create a mantra: "It's Just Parkinson's" (IJP). On days when your symptoms are minimal, it will roll off your tongue. The challenge will be saying it (and believing it) on your bad days, on the days when you can barely move, when just rolling over in bed feels Herculean.

But you've never been a quitter and I don't expect you to quit now. Whether in your past business ventures or your athletic endeavors, you've always had a never-give-up attitude. You've always made every effort when the outcome of a situation is in doubt. Embrace that mindset for it will serve you well.

Continue to laugh at yourself and at the situation you're in, for laughter truly is the best medicine.

As much as a positive attitude is therapeutic, never forget that one day you (we) will lose the battle with Parkinson's. I don't say this to be macabre or to have you lose hope. I know you'll never stop fighting since "surrender" is another word that's not in your vocabulary. I say this because knowledge is power. Don't be afraid to find out what's in store. Research PD in detail and learn from the experience of others, to get a better understanding of what the future may hold. Although everyone's journey is different, the more you know the better prepared you'll be. No sense in being caught off guard. Not knowing can be detrimental to your physical and mental health, so learn as much as you possibly can.

Not everything will change, not completely. You'll continue your athletic endeavors and take up Spartan obstacle course racing. It's a tough sport for a healthy person and formidable for a person with PD. But you'll do it! Next, you'll turn to powerlifting and you'll excel at it. To your great surprise, you'll discover powerlifting relieves many of your Parkinson's symptoms. A discovery that will fundamentally change your life—and possibly the lives of others.

There'll be many more activities you try along the way, such as wakeboarding, kite surfing and hiking. Some you'll master more than others, but the lesson is to never shy away from taking on new challenges. Don't believe the stereotypes of what someone with PD can or cannot do. Break the mold of what people expect of Parkinson's patients!

Don't take the people in your life for granted and count your blessings every day. You're fortunate to have your primary caregiver, Pattie, with you on every step of this journey. There will be others who come along down the road, let them in your life and allow them to help you. Don't be surprised if you enrich their lives as much as they enrich yours.

Besides your friends and loved ones, seek out experts and heed their advice. No one knows this disease better than a neurologist, so consult one early on and ask a lot of questions. Their knowledge of this disorder may ease some of your anxiety (especially in the early days of your diagnosis). Plus, they may recommend physical activities and training to help you navigate Parkinson's while staying fit. A therapist is also a must. Your emotional well-being is equally important to your physical health; you can't have one without the other.

In addition to regular exercise, a diet-based approach will do you good. Now more than ever, what you put into your body is important.

It's important not to think of Parkinson's as a life sentence. Although PD is incurable, you're still in control of your narrative. Face Parkinson's straight on and fight it with everything you have, as you've always done when obstacles come your way. You're still the warrior you've always been, you just have a different shield. In time you will come to say, and believe, *"I have Parkinson's, but Parkinson's doesn't have me."*

Love,
The Future John.

PS: WE got this. IJP.

Acknowledgements

Of all the chapters in *Unbreakable*, this one has been the most difficult to write. If I thanked everyone who influenced my life and therefore this book, I'd have to start the list with people I met as a child and finish with those I saw yesterday. Everybody, and I mean everybody, that I have ever met or known, has influenced this book one way or another. To those not mentioned in this section, I say thank you for your influence on this book. I apologize in advance, but there just wasn't enough space to name every single one of you. However, there are some people I'd like to specifically thank, as follows:

Pattie Stoffel – To say that you work hard supporting me is an extreme understatement. By just being you, you make every day of my life better, easier and more manageable. Your positive outlook and encouragement keep me going through even the darkest times. I surely know what it means to have a 'life partner'. Thank you for all you have done for me and thank you in advance for all you will do for me as Parkinson's takes more of me. Hang on for the ride of our lives. It's going to get curvy, but I know we will make it together.

Diana Nyad – To my all-time hero. I am humbled and honored that you wrote the forward for this book. I was floored when Diane contacted you and you remembered me 5 years after we met. I've used your mantra many times in my life as it is important to find a way through, over and around obstacles that impede your progress.

Mary Dartis – I'm certain that this book would not have been written without your superior writing abilities. At every turn you helped take my stories and ideas and integrate them into this wonderful book. I'm thankful we met during the making of *It's Just Parkinson's* the film. I'm also grateful that you made time for me to assist me in writing *Unbreakable*. Two projects that you made outstanding by participating in them

Diane Akam – You own my gratitude for pushing me to make the documentary *It's Just Parkinson's*. Without your tenacity in pushing the development of the movie, this book would have never materialized. Thank you for getting this book over the goal line. Your assistance in: getting editing done, the book cover design and getting the book published saved this project. I was floundering before you stepped in.

Ivan Suārez – Your support for all things IJP is phenomenal. More importantly, your support for me is second to none. As we know, Parkinson's can be a real mind fuck. You've seen me at some of my absolute lowest moments. Yet you never waver in your support and are always ready to jump in to shore me up. No matter what the situation. Finally, thank you for contributing to a kick-ass cover for *Unbreakable*.

Laurie Pasch – Over the last 15 years you have guided me through some of the toughest and most challenging times of my life. I truly don't know where I would be without you. Going forward, we will have much to work on together as I battle Parkinson's. Your wealth of knowledge was critical in the writing of Chapter 5 of this book. Without your input, the chapter would not have been as meaningful.

About the Author

John Cullen was born in Quantico, Virginia in 1959. As the son of a U.S. Marine Corps colonel, his family moved frequently during his childhood. Cullen later settled in Milwaukee, Wisconsin, where he raised his daughters, Mimi and Julia, and worked as the Chief Financial Officer for an online tech software company. After 20 years, he took early retirement in 2011. Four years later while cycling the Pyrenees in France, Cullen knew something was wrong. Upon his return to the United States, he was diagnosed with Parkinson's disease.

An avid athlete his whole life, John has participated in over 200 running and cycling races, and over a dozen obstacle races. Cullen has slowly had to relinquish many of these athletic pursuits due to Parkinson's. In 2019 he started powerlifting. To his surprise, he discovered that lifting heavy weights stressed his central nervous system, which helped set back some of his Parkinson's symptoms.

In 2019 Cullen created the mantra, "It's Just Parkinson's" (IJP), the philosophy he uses as he battles this incurable disease.

In 2021, this mindset led to the feature-length documentary *It's Just Parkinson's*, which chronicles Cullen's journey living with Parkinson's and the importance of this IJP mindset to survive adversity. The documentary highlights the discovery that powerlifting dramatically improves his mobility. The film has been featured in several North American film festivals and has inspired individuals from all walks of life.

The Instagram account @itsjustparkinsons cultivates a worldwide community of individuals with an IJP mindset and is growing each day.

A role model to many, Cullen is a sought-after media source and public speaker. He lives in Sanibel, Florida with his loving partner Pattie.

Visit www.itsjustparkinsons.com to watch Cullen's documentary *It's Just Parkinson's*.

About the Logo

In Greek mythology, Atlas was the Titan god condemned to hold up the heavens for all eternity, and he is depicted as holding a large sphere on his shoulders.

Atlas symbolizes the endurance and strength of people who have been diagnosed with Parkinson's, and the tremendous amount of weight they must carry while battling this incurable disease.

The IJP logo was designed by Kevin Taylor as a tribute to his father, who battled Parkinson's. It shows Atlas holding up those three letters I-J-P. It's a reminder that even when you feel that you have the weight of the world on your shoulders, you need to keep lifting, stay strong, and never stop fighting.

The IJP warrior mindset can be summarized with three words: ROCK - LIGHT - HOPE. Our mission is to provide support, raise awareness, and promote a positive outlook for individuals living with Parkinson's disease. We recognize the challenges faced by those affected by Parkinson's and aim to create a community that fosters hope, resilience, and empowerment.

www.ingramcontent.com/pod-product-compliance
Lightning Source LLC
Chambersburg PA
CBHW051535120626
46551CB00012B/1238